Recipes from the Dairy

Cookery books published by the National Trust

National Trust Recipes by Sarah Edington

Healthy Eating by Sarah Edington

Teatime Recipes by Jane Pettigrew

Picnics by Kate Crookenden, Margaret Willes and Caroline Worlledge

The Art of Dining by Sara Paston-Williams

A Book of Historical Recipes by Sara Paston-Williams

Recipes from the Dairy

Robin Weir and Caroline Liddell
with Peter Brears

Special Photography by Andreas von Einsiedel

The National Trust

Distributed by
Trafalgar Square
North Pomfret, Vermont 05053

First published in Great Britain in 1998 by
National Trust Enterprises Ltd
36 Queen Anne's Gate
London SW1H 9AS

British Library Cataloguing in Publication Data
A catalogue record for this book is available from the British Library

ISBN 0 7078 0243 1

Designed by the Newton Engert Partnership

Phototypeset in ITC Berkeley Oldstyle

Printed and bound in Great Britain by Butler & Tanner Ltd

Contents

To Elizabeth, Charlotte and Matthew

Introduction

Although the English country house dairy played an important role in the self sufficiency of large estates, there are surprisingly few references to methods of work and techniques, since these were passed down through the generations by word of mouth and rarely written down. Moreover, although the English diet has always been based on dairy foods and meat, many of the classic dairy recipes have either been forgotten or developed to such a point as to be unrecognisable in their modern adaptation. Where tastes have changed or old ingredients cannot be easily obtained, we have brought these recipes up to date. Fortunately there has been a recent revival of interest in traditional dishes, and hopefully more will appear on menus in the future.

You will find references in the book to whole milk in which case full-fat/non-skimmed milk should be used. Likewise single or double cream should not be used where whipping/heavy cream is specified. Never use longlife or artificially thickened milk or cream. Where we mention sugar without specifying type, we recommend using unrefined granulated.

The National Trust has some wonderful dairies and ice-houses, many of them open to the public, and there is a list of these at the end of the book. But it was the dairy at Ham House in Surrey with its extraordinary cow's legs that provided the inspiration for this book. We should like to thank Jan Graffius and her colleagues at Ham for allowing us to take photographs in the dairy, including our cover picture. We are delighted that plans are afoot to open it to the public when funds are available.

The shots of food in the book were taken at Syon House, home of the Dukes of Northumberland on the banks of the Thames not far from Ham. We are grateful to his Grace, the Duke of Northumberland and Richard Pailthorpe, Louise Taylor and Steven Lovegrove for allowing us to use the wonderful confectioner's kitchen and dining room for the photography. We also thank Andreas von Einsiedel for his inspired photographs.

Others who must be thanked for their help in the production of the book are Chris Bird of the Product Research Centre at Reaseheath, Janet Clark, Ivan Day, Penny Hatfield, Grace Mulligan, Malcolm Thick, Sara Paston-Williams, Paddi Rogers and Theodore Zeldin. Thank you too to Gail Engert for her design, Morwenna Wallis at the National Trust for her help, advice and coordinating role, Jane Judd, our agent, and finally to Margaret Willes, the Trust's Publisher, for her patience and long suffering during the lengthy birth of the book.

Part One

THE DAIRY

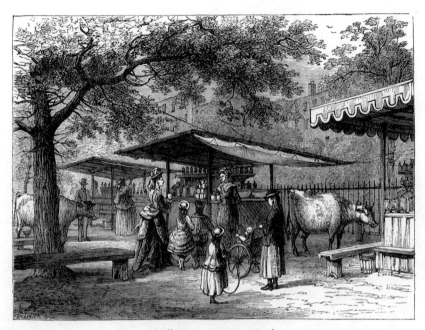

Milk Fair, St James's Park

Dairying has always been a feminine activity. The very word 'dairy' comes from the Middle English, 'dey' meaning a serving woman, and 'erie', the place of her work. Here, according to Thomas Lodge and Robert Greene in *A Looking Glasse for London and England*, published in 1598, she made her 'butter, cheese, whay, curds, creame, sod [boiled] milke, raw-milke, sower-milke, sweet-milke, and butter milke'.

For centuries the dairymaid's day started at dawn. Sir Thomas Overbury, in *Characters*, written in the early seventeenth century, explains 'she doth not, with lying a-bed long spoil her complexion … she rises therefore with Chanticleer [the cockerel] her dame's clock, and at night makes the lamb her curfew'.

Carrying her pail and stool she went into the pasture, slipped a soft plaited rope around the cow's hind legs, a wooden toggle looped through one end holding it in place, so the animal could neither kick nor walk away while being milked. The three-legged milking stool would stand firm on even ground, as she tucked her pail beneath the cow to draw the milk. Once the pail was full, she lifted it on to the top of her head, steadying it with one hand as she returned to the dairy.

Pure milk, rich cream, fine and well-flavoured butter and cheeses have always formed an essential part of the diet, whether consumed fresh or as raw ingredients in all manner of recipes. Today we tend to take these ingredients for granted, for they are readily available in almost unlimited quantities, regardless of the season or where we live and strict hygiene regulations and large-scale processing ensure they contain no impurities detrimental to our health. It is only during the twentieth century, however, that we have achieved this transformation. Before then, the only way to ensure a good supply of dairy products was to keep one's own herd of cows and employ a dairymaid to transform their milk into clean, wholesome comestibles.

The dairymaid's first task was to ensure no contamination from the hair or skin of the cow by pouring the milk through a sieve of freshly laundered muslin. Then she began to extract the cream. This was usually done by pouring milk into bowls of wood or pottery, and leaving them in a cool place for perhaps a day. By that time the cream had risen to form a thick layer that could be lifted off using shallow, perforated 'flets', and placed within a clean cream pot. From about 1800 shallow rectangular trays were used for this purpose, some of lead, others of fine slate extracted from the famous quarries of Mr Hind at Swithland in Leicestershire, or Lord Penrhyn in North Wales. Each had a tall tapered plug set into its flat base so that the milk could be slowly run off, leaving the cream to be scooped up with a cream-knife, perhaps made of ivory.

In Devon and Cornwall a completely different method was used for making cream. The milk stood overnight in cream pans of beaten brass, which were then placed on hot cinders, or over specially made stoves, until a ring of cream rose in the centre. After spending a second night in the cool of the dairy, it had transformed itself into a thick, slightly smoke-flavoured clotted cream, for which this area of England is famous. In the dairy at Lanhydrock in Cornwall, rebuilt after a disastrous fire in 1881, a scalding range was installed in the scullery. It was built on

Plunge-churn for butter making

10

the inner wall of the house and heated very gently by hot-water pipes from the boiler-house in the cellar below. This slow-burning range brought the clotted cream to perfection.

Once the cream was ready, the dairymaid could send supplies of milk and cream up to the house. She now turned to the making of butter and cheese. Usually she poured the cream into a tall coopered plunge-churn, and then inserted a flat, round dasher, pierced with numerous holes and mounted on a long wooden shaft. This was worked regularly up and down, keeping the milk in a state of perpetual agitation. More haste certainly did mean less speed.

> If you want your butter both nice and sweet
> Don't churn with nervous jerking,
> But ply the dasher slowly and neat,
> You'll hardly know you are working,
> And when the butter is coming you'll say,
> 'Yes, surely, this is the better way' –
> Churn slowly!
>
> *Farm, Field and Fireside*, 15 June 1888

By the middle of the eighteenth century butter was churned in barrels turned by hand on a horizontal axis, with paddles mounted around their inner surfaces regularly beating the milk. There was a variety of box-churns too, which had dashers

Barrel-churn for butter making

rotating inside their square- or barrel-shaped bodies. After some time – many hours if the weather was either too hot or too cold – the butter began to form, first into globules, and then into lumps which could be removed from the churn with wooden scoops. In the West Country butter-churns were rarely used, for here the clotted cream was put into a broad shallow milk-tub and agitated with the flat of the hand; this handmade butter was always considered superior in flavour to that made with raw cream.

The water acidic butter-milk remaining in the churn was a great delicacy in Henry VIII's England, for 'Nothyng nourisheth more than this mylke whan hit is newe, sopped up with newe hotte breadde', according to T. Pagnell in *Schola Salernitana Regimen Sanitatis Salerni*, published in 1528. Alternatively, the addition of new hot milk produced both curds and whey, or whig, an excellent cool drink in summer. Curds were eaten with cream, ale or wine, as Miss Muffet probably did, or were made into cheesecakes. As butter-milk soon decayed, it was essential that every trace was removed from the butter; this was done by placing the butter in a clean wooden or earthenware bowl with clean water and beating it with the hand until every trace had been extracted. If fresh butter was required for the house, it was now beaten into blocks with wooden paddles called 'Scotch hands', or made up into round pats. Butter needed for winter use was beaten down into pots or wooden firkins with plenty of salt to keep it in good condition.

In most dairies cheese was made from either whole milk or the skimmed milk left after removing the cream. First, it was poured into a huge brass pan called a cheese-kettle and hung over the fire until it was at blood temperature. Rennet, the natural enzyme from the preserved stomach of a calf, was added to transform the milk into a soft junket-like curd. Placed in a shallow dish, the curd was then broken up and gently pressed to the bottom of the kettle, so that the liquid whey could be removed.

The next task was to line a cheese-vat (made like a cylindrical barrel with the top missing and the walls and base drilled with numerous small holes) with a piece of muslin. Once this had been filled with the curds, a shallow wooden plug, or sinker, was placed on top and a weight added, slowly to squeeze out the surplus whey and form a moist, crumbly cheese. In this state it would soon go bad, so it was then wrapped in new muslin, returned to the cheese-vat, and placed under a really heavy pressure in a cheese-press to extract virtually all the whey and leave a firm hard cheese. These presses varied enormously in design, some exerting their pressure by huge stone weights, others by long levers or by screw devices.

Once the cheese had been thoroughly pressed, perhaps for a day or more, it was removed from the vat, probably rubbed with salt or brine, and set on the shelves of a cool cheese-room, where it was regularly turned until it had dried out and matured ready for use. The final flavour depended on many things – the nature of the soil, the food eaten by the cows, their breed, the time of the year, the techniques used by the dairymaid, and her experience and skill. In the seventeenth century the farms of Suffolk and Essex, for instance, enjoyed a poor reputation for hard cheeses, probably because butter took priority. A rhyme of the period ran:

> Those that made me were uncivil;
> They made me harder than the devil,
> Knives won't cut me, fire won't sweat me,
> Dogs bark at me, but can't eat me

On 4 October 1661 Samuel Pepys noted in his diary that on his return home from the theatre he found 'my wife vexed at her people [servants] for grumbling to eate Suffolk cheese – which I also am vexed at.' An earlier reference described a much more cheerful encounter with a Cheshire cheese. The development of cheese-fairs, merchants and mongers heralded the fine range of regional cheeses from Cheddar, Gloucester and Cheshire that we still recognise and appreciate today.

Stiltons, sometimes called British Parmesan, were made in May or June and stored until early December when they were ripened for serving at Christmas. This was best done naturally, but could be induced by cutting a small hole in the top, and inserting a piece of well-matured Cheshire cheese, while some households preferred to pour in port, sherry, Madeira or old ale.

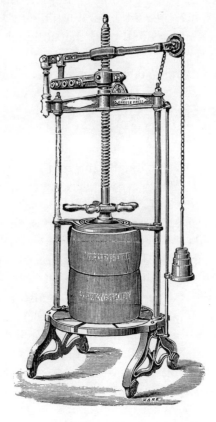

Cheese-press

In addition to hard cheese, there was a fine tradition of making rich cream cheeses. Plain ones were made by simply adding a little salt to the cream and moulding it on napkins, a calf's bladder, or wrapping it in fresh nettle leaves.

The traditional dairy usually formed part of the farm buildings or, in smaller establishments, it occupied an outbuilding attached to the main house. It was essentially a practical workplace, with whitewashed walls, and a series of wooden or slate workbenches and shelves fitted around the walls. Ideally it had a pump or other source of clean fresh water nearby, along with a large built-in boiling copper to heat the water for scalding and scouring all the worktops and utensils, for any dirt would soon spoil the taste and appearance of dairy produce. Keeping everything really clean took a great deal of time and energy. One Stuart dairymaid pointed out that 'she had to milke, scalde milk pannes, wash the cherne and butter dishes, ring up a cheese clout, and set everything in good order.'

Many dairies operated in this way well into the twentieth century. Good examples are still to be seen, such as at Townend, at Troutbeck in Cumbria, the establishment of a 'statesman' farming family.

The clean, healthy, outdoor life which gave the dairymaid her beauty, happiness and modesty was celebrated by poets through the centuries. So prevalent was the view that dairymaids followed an exemplary lifestyle that gentlemen felt it was one their wives and daughters would do well to imitate. Henry Percy, 9th Earl of Northumberland had to admit, around 1600, that although 'The kitchen, buttery or pantry are not places for [great men's wyfes], the dairy is tolerable; for soe may yow have perhaps a disch of butter, a soft cheese or somme clouted creme in a summer.'

For the wives' benefit, seventeenth-century cookery writers provided a wealth of instructions and recipes, but the real boost to the genteel dairymaid fashion came in the 1690s when Queen Mary set up her own dairy at Hampton Court Palace, furnishing it with the finest Delftware milk-bowls, their white glossy glazes decorated in cobalt blue brushwork. By the mid-eighteenth century, when the Romantic movement invaded every aspect of art, literature and life, ladies as grand as George III's Queen, Charlotte, and the Duchesses of Norfolk, Bedford and Rutland, were all taking a great interest in their dairies and personal dairying skills.

Being a noble dairymaid rarely required carrying out the full range of dairymaid's duties; something much more elegant had to be created. Prince Pückler-Muskau, who came to England in the 1830s, commented: 'I told you once before that the dairy is one of the principal decorations of an English park and stands by itself, quite away from the cow-house. It is generally an elegant pavilion adorned with fountains, marble walls, rare and beautiful porcelain and its vessels large and small filled with exquisite milk and its products in all their varieties.'

Architects designed these pleasure-ground dairies in the latest style. The most popular was classical, as at Petworth in Sussex for the Wyndhams, and Shugborough in Staffordshire for the Ansons. At Woburn the Duchess of Bedford adopted the Chinese style, at Sezincote in Oxfordshire the dairy was Moorish, while Gothic was deemed appropriate for Wimpole Hall in Cambridgeshire designed by Sir John Soane. The rustic style proved particularly suitable because the insulation and deep, shady eaves of thatched roofs ensured that the dairy remained cool even on the hottest summer's day. John Nash's octagonal dairy at Blaise Castle near Bristol is perhaps the finest example of this genre.

On entering a dairy, there were often a few steps down, as the marble, slate, stone or tiled floor was sunk into the soil to keep the space cool. The walls were usually covered in glazed ceramic tiles, perhaps in pale cream, with beautifully hand-painted ivy tendril borders, as supplied by Wedgwood for Uppark in Sussex, Ham in Surrey, and Althorp in Northamptonshire, or in the most delicate green and cream that the company made for the exquisite dairy at Berrington Hall in Hereford and Worcester. Dutch tiles were popular too, their cobalt blue or manganese purple-painted roundels always looking fresh and neat, as at Dyrham Park in Gloucesterhire. Lady Anson's dairy at Shugborough was sheathed in Derbyshire alabaster, but this probably survived from the building's earlier use as a garden pavilion. In the finer dairies, the flood of sunlight was reduced by filling the windows with panels of etched or stained glass, but most relied on wide eaves and verandas for the purpose.

Cool worktops were provided by marble or slate benches set on rows of brackets, marble Doric columns, or, as at Ham House, the striking cast-iron cow's legs. Regimented rows of milk-pans were set out here, while niches in the walls might have held Neo-classical cream-pots. These were virtually a Wedgwood monopoly in the late Georgian period, often being made to match the wall-tiles, but Minton and other Staffordshire manufacturers went on to produce excellent ceramics for Victorian lady dairymaids. In addition to these basic facilities, there might be

wall-shelves for fine porcelain, internal fountains to cool the air and delight the ear, and tea-rooms and porticoed verandas to entertain one's friends after skimming a milk-pan or making a cream cheese.

There was often a back door, too, which led into a working dairy scullery, where the farm dairymaids completed their daily tasks and cleaned up after the ladies had departed from the front dairy. This close contact between family and servant areas could lead to surprising events, as when Sir Harry Fetherstonhaugh, squire of Uppark, proposed to Mary Ann Bullock, his dairymaid in 1825. She was 'taken aback like', but he told her to signal her consent by cutting a slice out of the leg of mutton planned for dinner that evening. The slice was cut and she went on to become mistress of this great Sussex house for almost half a century.

Georgian romanticism, however, gave way to Victorian practicality. During the years of farming prosperity between 1850 and about 1870 many landowners built new model dairies on their farms. The finest of these was built by Prince Albert in the park at Windsor. Typical of this period, it combines the highest quality of design with real practicality. The 'show' dairy, which visitors would first inspect, has a large mermaid fountain at one end, water cascading from her clam-shell bowl into aquamarine tiled channels. These flow beneath pristine white marble benches supporting 114 pear-shaped Minton china cream-settling pans arranged in rows, ensuring that the 240 gallons of milk they contained remained cool and clean. Cavity walls sheathed in glossy Minton polychrome tiles, a ventilating turret on the roof, double-glazed windows and the most brilliant of Victorian stained glass complete a truly magnificent interior. Adjoining this was the dairy scullery, where all the other practical aspects of dairywork could be completed, using all the most efficient and up-to-date equipment.

Many nobles and gentlemen built similar model dairies but none could match Albert's great achievement at Windsor. Perhaps Disraeli had it in mind when writing *Tothair*: 'A pretty sight is a first-rate dairy, with its floor in fanciful tiles and its cool shrouded chambers, its stained glass windows and its marble slabs, and porcelain pots of cream and plenteous platters of fantastically formed butter.'

By the 1850s landowners had begun to invest in a variety of new equipment to ensure that their dairies maintained the highest standards. In the 1880s dairy thermometers were introduced, but the dairymaids looked on them as useless ornaments, preferring to rely on their own judgement of temperature when making cheese. Other inventions were readily adopted, however, for their benefits

Opposite: A 19th-century coloured stipple engraving
of a milkmaid at Polesden Lacey, Surrey.
(*NTPL/Derrick E. Witty*)

Jersey Creamer

were obvious. These included the Jersey Creamer, an efficient settling pan which delighted the Prince and Princess of Wales at Sandringham, whose dairymaid reported: 'there is about twice as much cream as I should get off the pans with the old system.' The De Laval Centrifugal Cream Separator, introduced at the Royal Agricultural Show at Kilburn in West London in 1879, really did extract 15 per cent more cream from the milk and became extremely popular.

The new Victoria barrel-churn invented by William Wade of Leeds did away with dashers by tumbling its barrel 'end over end', and was soon installed in the dairy at Windsor. At the same time a variety of butter-workers made redundant the tiresome old hand-beating process, the butter being laid in a shallow wooden trough with a longitudinal or spiral-grooved roller passed across it, squeezing out the butter-milk, mixing in the salt and compacting it ready for packing.

In some great houses, such as Petworth, further refinements were made in the early twentieth century, when the cow-yard dairy close to the house was closed down and replaced with separate model dairies, each serving a particular breed of cattle on a nearby tenant farm. Here was real sophistication, for now guests might be approached at tea by footmen who could enquire, 'Milk or cream, Madam?' and, on receiving the appropriate answer, could next enquire, 'Shorthorn or Guernsey, Madam?'

Opposite: Lanhydrock Dairy showing the marble cooling table, with a groove for cold, running water.
(*NTPL/Andreas von Einsiedel*)

Chapter 1
HORS D'OEUVRES AND SOUPS

Table setting à la russe

The term *hors d'oeuvres* comes from the French and literally means out of the ordinary course of things. Gastronomically, hors d'oeuvres represent an extra course at the beginning of the meal, and came into their own in Britain in the nineteenth century when a revolution took place in the style of dining.

For centuries the style had been *à la française* with dishes brought to the table simultaneously in two main courses, sometimes supplemented by a third known as the banquet or later as the dessert. Before the diners arrived at the table, servants would have laid the dishes for the first course in a symmetrical style on the table with the soup at one end and the fish at the other to be served by the host and hostess. Once seated, diners helped themselves to the dishes nearest to them – and there was little chance that they might be hot.

The custom of Russian society, however, was to have the table laid with complete place settings, and to have courses handed round by servants – with a fighting chance of hot food reaching the table. This idea, known as dining *à la russe*, was introduced to Paris in 1810 by the Russian Ambassador, and gradually took hold in Britain, at first for grand occasions. By the 1860s most homes of fashion served food in this manner, often providing hors d'oeuvres as the opening course.

Potted kippers

In the eighteenth century both salmon and herring were 'kippered', or preserved by the drying and smoking process. Today kipper refers only to herrings.

This recipe will work with almost any smoked fish, such as bloaters, mackerel or trout. However, if using smoked salmon choose the cheaper off-cuts and, of course, it does not need the initial frying. For a smooth texture use a food processor, but if you would prefer a flaked texture, beat the cooked fish with a fork. The potted paste will keep for up to two weeks in a fridge if the butter seal is left intact.

Metric	US	Imperial	
75g	¾ stick	3oz	*Unsalted butter*
400g	14oz	14oz	*Kipper fillets, boned*
325ml	1¼ cups	10fl oz	*Whipping/heavy cream*
2–3 tsp	2–3 tsp	2–3 tsp	*Lemon juice*
			Chilli-flavoured vinegar
Makes about			
750ml	3 cups	24fl oz	

Heat 2 tablespoons of the butter in a frying pan. When the butter is frothy lay the kipper fillets, flesh side down, in the pan. Fry over a moderate heat for about 2 minutes, then turn and fry for a further 2 minutes. Remove the pan from the heat.

Scrape off and discard the black skin from the fillets. Transfer the kippers and all the buttery pan juices to a processor and blend until smooth.

In a separate bowl beat the cream until it just holds a shape, then stir about 2 tablespoons into the kipper mixture to loosen it. Now fold the kippers and cream together, taste and season carefully with lemon juice and a dash of chilli-flavoured vinegar. Spread the mixture into a small lidded dish or individual ramekins, smooth the surface with a knife and refrigerate until firm.

Melt the remaining butter and spoon over the surface to form a butter seal. Chill until ready to serve. Best served with fingers of hot toast or Melba toast.

Chilled cucumber and fresh herb mousse

Metric	US	Imperial	
900g	2lb	2lb	Cucumbers (approx. 2)
2 tbsp	2 tbsp	2 tbsp	Salt
125ml	½ cup	4 fl oz	Chicken stock
25g	25g	25g	Gelatine
450g	1lb	1lb	Curd cheese
2	2	2	Spring onions, trimmed and finely chopped
2 tbsp	2 tbsp	2 tbsp	Snipped chives
1½ tbsp	1½ tbsp	1½ tbsp	Mint, freshly chopped
1 tbsp	1 tbsp	1 tbsp	Wine vinegar
125ml	½ cup	4 fl oz	Whipping/heavy cream
			Salt and freshly ground black pepper

Makes enough to fill

1·3 litre mould	5½ cup mould	45 fl oz mould

Grate the cucumbers into a colander, sprinkling with salt as you go. Place a plate over the cucumber, and compress with a jar or can on top. Leave to drain for 30 minutes.

Bring the chicken stock to the boil in a small pan and remove from the heat. Sprinkle in the gelatine and whisk to mix. Leave aside, stirring occasionally until cool. In a large bowl, beat the curd cheese until smooth, then beat in the cooled chicken stock, cucumber, onions, chives, herbs and wine vinegar.

In a separate small bowl beat the cream until stiff enough to hold a shape, then fold in the cucumber mixture. Season to taste and pour the mixture into the oiled mould. Cover with cling-film and leave overnight in the fridge to set.

When ready to serve, dip the mould into hot water to the count of ten, then unmould on to a plate. Fill the centre of the cucumber mousse with a green salad tossed in a garlicky vinaigrette. Serve lightly chilled.

The cucumber mousse can also be moulded in individual ramekins and served on small plates surrounded by green salad.

Spinach-dressed eggs in cases

Metric	US	Imperial	
350g	12oz	12oz	Fresh spinach, prepared and washed
200ml	¾ cup	6fl oz	Single/light cream
125g	1 cup	4oz	Parmesan cheese, grated
			Squeeze of lemon juice
			Salt and freshly ground black pepper
6	6	6	Eggs
6	6	6	Baked pastry cases, 10cm/4in round and 2·5cm/1in deep

Preheat the oven to 180°C/350°F/gas mark 4/FO 160°C.

Put the wet spinach in a pan with a sprinkling of salt. Cook over a moderate heat, stirring occasionally until it wilts and forms a soft mass, about 4–5 minutes. Drain in a colander and leave until it is cool enough to handle. Squeeze the excess liquid from the spinach, then put the leaves in a bowl with 4–5 tablespoons of cream and the Parmesan cheese. Beat together, then season to taste with lemon juice, salt and freshly ground black pepper.

Arrange the six pastry cases on a baking tray and spoon some of the spinach mixture into the base of each tartlet. Break an egg into each one, spoon the remaining cream over the top and sprinkle with the remaining cheese. Bake for 12–15 minutes, or until the eggs have just set and the yolks remain runny. Serve immediately with a green salad of peppery-flavoured leaves.

A nice whet before dinner

This recipe comes from Elizabeth Raffald's very successful cookery book, *The Experienced English Housekeeper*, first published in 1769. We have left Mrs Raffald's title because, although the word 'whet' is rarely used, it is a nice description. Think of it quite simply as whetting the appetite – to get the gastric juices flowing. Not for faint-hearted anchovy-lovers.

Metric	US	Imperial	
4	4	4	Brown or white bread slices
50g	2oz	2oz	Anchovies, canned
50g	½ stick	2oz	Butter
110g	1 cup	4oz	Cheshire cheese, grated
2 tbsp	2 tbsp	2 tbsp	Parsley sprigs, chopped
			Black pepper, freshly ground

Serves one passionate anchovy lover or four as an appetite whetter.

Remove the crusts from the bread if you prefer. Drain the oil from the anchovies into a large frying pan. Add the butter to the oil and heat until melted and bubbling. Fry the bread slowly on both sides so that the slices become crisp and pale golden.

Line a grill pan with foil and arrange the fried bread on top. Lay two anchovies across each piece.

Combine the grated cheese with the chopped parsley and some pepper. Strew thickly over the bread pieces and grill until bubbling. Cut into squares, and serve piping hot.

Mrs Raffald recommends drizzling it with additional butter.

Cheddar cheese and vegetable soup

A wonderful warming and unctuous soup, ideal for cold weather. The flavour depends largely on the quality of the cheese; nothing less than a mature, rinded English Cheddar will do. This splendid soup does have one drawback: once the cheese has been added, it must not be boiled, so if the soup needs to be reheated, use a heat-diffuser mat under the pan.

Metric	US	Imperial	
75g	¾ stick	3oz	*Butter*
2 medium	½ cup	2 medium	*Carrots, peeled and finely chopped*
2 medium	½ cup	2 medium	*Celery stalks, scrubbed and finely chopped*
1	½ cup	1	*Spanish onion, peeled and finely chopped*
¼	2 cups	¼	*Savoy cabbage, washed and shredded*
3 tbsp	3 tbsp	3 tbsp	*Fine oatmeal*
1 litre	4 cups	35 fl oz	*Chicken stock*
450 ml	1¾ cups	14 fl oz	*Whole milk*
200g	3 cups	7oz	*Mature Cheddar, grated*
			Salt and freshly ground black pepper
			Chopped parsley to garnish
Makes about			
1·6 litres	6½ cups	55 fl oz	

Melt the butter in a large deep pan. When bubbling hot, add the carrots, celery and onion. Cook for 5 minutes without browning, then stir in the cabbage and cook for a further 3 minutes. Sprinkle in the oatmeal, stir and cook for one minute. Don't worry if the oatmeal forms a crust on the base of the pan.

Add the stock and bring to the boil, still stirring, and the oatmeal on the base will blend evenly into the soup. Simmer uncovered for about 5 minutes, or until the vegetables are tender. Now pour in the milk and bring back to the boil before removing the pan from the heat. Stir in the cheese, and when melted, taste and season with salt and freshly ground black pepper.

Garnish and serve immediately with brown bread.

Jugged green pea soup

Metric	US	Imperial	
900 g	2 lb	2 lb	Fresh peas, shelled
1 tbsp	1 tbsp	1 tbsp	Butter
¼–½ tsp	¼–½ tsp	¼–½ tsp	Sugar
			Salt and freshly ground black pepper
approx. 12	approx. 12	approx. 12	Mint leaves
750 ml	3 cups	24 fl oz	Chicken stock
250 ml	1 cup	8 fl oz	Single/light cream
			Generous squeeze of lemon juice
Makes about			
1·5 litres	6 cups	50 fl oz	

Put the peas into a 1·5 litre/6 cup/48 fl oz preserving jar, layering them with the butter, sugar, seasoning and mint leaves. Close tightly and stand the jar in a deep stockpot filled with sufficient water to come two-thirds of the way up the side of the jar. Bring to a simmer and cook, uncovered, for 30 minutes.

Empty the contents of the preserving jar into a food-processor and blend for about 3 minutes. With the machine still in motion, gradually add about half the stock, or as much as the capacity of the machine can cope with.

Rub the purée through a sieve into a pan, add the remaining stock and cream, then reheat the mixture.

Season to taste, balancing the sugar, lemon juice, salt and freshly ground black pepper to your liking. Serve hot.

Celery, white wine and Stilton soup

Metric	US	Imperial	
50g	½ stick	2oz	Butter
1 large	1 large	1 large	Spanish onion, peeled and finely chopped
3	3	3	Celery stalks, scrubbed, trimmed and finely chopped
50g	⅓ cup	2oz	Plain white flour
325ml	1¼ cups	10fl oz	Whole milk
1 litre	4 cups	32fl oz	Chicken stock
325ml	1¼ cups	10fl oz	Dry white wine
150g	2 cups	5oz	Stilton cheese, crumbled
100ml	⅓ cup	3fl oz	Whipping/heavy cream
			Generous squeeze of lemon juice
			Salt and freshly ground black pepper
			GARNISH:
			Fresh celery leaves, chopped

Makes about

2 litres	8 cups	65fl oz

In a large pan heat the butter until melted and frothy. Stir in the onion and celery, then cover and cook over a low heat for about 10 minutes or until slightly softened, but not coloured.

Stir in the flour and continue to cook for a minute or so before gradually stirring in the milk. Bring to the boil, then leave to simmer, uncovered, for 5–10 minutes or until the vegetables are soft.

Add the stock and the wine, bring the soup to just below boiling point, then remove the pan from the heat. Whisk the cheese into the soup and when melted add the cream. Season to taste with lemon juice, salt and freshly ground black pepper.

Garnish with chopped fresh celery leaves. Serve with oatcakes.

White onion soup

Everyone has become so used to French onion soup that white onion soup has been all but forgotten.

Metric	US	Imperial	
3 large	3 large	3 large	*Spanish onions, peeled and sliced*
1 litre	4 cups	32 fl oz	*Chicken stock*
2-3	2-3	2-3	*Blades of mace*
			Salt and ground white pepper
25g	¼ stick	1oz	*Butter*
25g	2 tbsp	1oz	*Plain white flour*
150 ml	¾ cup	5 fl oz	*Single/light cream*
½-1 tsp	½-1 tsp	½-1 tsp	*Sugar*
			Squeeze of lemon juice
			GARNISH:
3-4 tbsp	3-4 tbsp	3-4 tbsp	*Olive oil*
25g	¼ cup	1oz	*Walnuts, shelled*
4-5 sprigs	4-5 sprigs	4-5 sprigs	*Parsley*
1	1	1	*Garlic clove, peeled*
Makes about			
1·5 litres	6 cups	50 fl oz	

Put the onions, stock, mace and a little salt and pepper seasoning in a large pan and bring to simmering point. Cover and cook gently for 10-15 minutes or until the onions are tender. Remove the pan from the heat and leave until the contents are cool.

Strain the onions, reserving the liquid. Discard the mace. Purée the onions, either by processing or rubbing through a sieve. Return the rinsed-out pan to the heat and melt the butter. Stir in the flour, then, working over a moderate heat, gradually add the reserved stock and bring to the boil, stirring all the time. Leave to boil gently for 2-3 minutes, then add the onion purée and cream. Taste and flavour with sugar, lemon juice and seasoning.

While the soup reheats, prepare the garnish by briefly sautéing the nuts in 1 tablespoon of oil until lightly toasted. Then liquidise, or pound together with a pestle and mortar, with the remaining ingredients, adding a little more oil if necessary to form a thin paste. Swirl a small amount into each serving of soup.

Lady Murray's white soup

A recipe loosely adapted from the *Cook Book of Lady Clark of Tillypronie*. Given that this book was published in 1909, it is not surprising that the recipes reflect Edwardian sensibilities, but this soup is 'old-fashioned' in the nicest possible way. Don't be put off by the apparent simplicity of the ingredients. The resulting soup is of a standard and style with which we have lost touch, and that is our loss.

Metric	US	Imperial	
1	1	1	Rabbit, jointed
1 litre	4 cups	32 fl oz	Chicken stock
			A handful of parsley stalks
50 g	¼ cup	2 oz	Pearl barley
500 ml	2 cups	16 fl oz	Whole milk
2 tbsp	2 tbsp	2 tbsp	Capers, drained and chopped
110 g	1 cup	4 oz	Cooked peas or asparagus tips
125 ml	½ cup	4 fl oz	Single/light cream
			Generous squeeze of lemon juice
			Salt and ground white pepper

Makes about			
1·5 litres	6 cups	50 fl oz	

Put the rabbit joints, stock and parsley stalks in a large pan and bring to the boil.

Meanwhile, put the barley in a sieve; rinse, then put in a small pan and cover with cold water. Bring to the boil, strain and add to the pan with the rabbit. As soon as the liquid returns to the boil, adjust the heat to give a gentle simmer, cover and cook for 2 hours or until the rabbit falls easily from the bones and the barley grains are tender.

Drain the contents of the pan into a large sieve set over a bowl. Remove the meat and strip from the bones. Put the meat and the rest of the contents of the sieve into a food processor and reduce to a paste. Put this into the rinsed-out pan, then add the strained stock and the milk and reheat.

As soon as the soup reaches a serving temperature, add the capers, vegetables, cream and lemon juice and season to taste. Serve hot.

Chapter 2

SUPPER DISHES

To dress macaroni with Parmesan cheese

This recipe is adapted from Mrs Raffald's *The Experienced English Housekeeper*, published in 1769. It is the forerunner of our macaroni cheese and was written when items such as dried macaroni or *maccheroni*, vermicelli and olive oil from Lucca were highly prized foods imported by Italian warehousemen, many of whom had shops and warehouses in central London. *Maccheroni* first appeared in Italy in 1279 and in England at the beginning of the sixteenth century. It was made by rolling thinned-out dough around knitting needles. It would have been sold in lengths which were broken into smaller pieces before cooking. However, the modern, short variety is much easier to prepare and to eat.

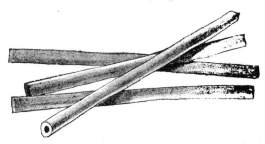

In the original recipe the cooked pasta had cream poured over it and was then dressed with toasted Parmesan cheese. Mrs Raffald suggested that it be sent 'to the table on a water plate, for it soon goes cold', which is very true.

Metric	US	Imperial	
400g	14oz	14oz	*Short cut, small bore macaroni*
			Salt
325ml	1¼ cups	10fl oz	*Single/light cream*
35g	3 tbsp	1½oz	*Butter, softened*
35g	3 tbsp	1½oz	*Plain white flour*
325ml	1¼ cups	10fl oz	*Whole milk*
110g	1 cup	4oz	*Mature Cheddar cheese, grated*
			White pepper
75g	⅔ cup	2½oz	*Parmesan cheese, grated*

Preheat the oven to 200°C/400°F/gas mark 6/FO 180°C.

Cook the macaroni in plenty of boiling salted water for at least 5 minutes less than the packet instructions. Drain and rinse with cold water. Turn the pasta on to a double thickness of kitchen paper, cover with a towel and leave aside while you are making the sauce.

Pour the cream into a medium-size pan and start to warm gently.

In a small bowl, combine the butter and flour to form a paste, and add small pieces to the warming cream as you stir. Bring to the boil, still stirring, then once the sauce is thickened and bubbling, add the milk and leave to boil gently for 5 minutes.

Remove the pan from the heat and stir in the Cheddar cheese. Season strongly, then fold in the drained pasta. Mix thoroughly then spread in a thickly buttered gratin dish. Cover with the Parmesan cheese and bake for about 25 minutes, or until bubbling and golden. Serve piping hot.

Good with grilled bacon rolls and tomatoes.

Ramekins of baked eggs, bacon and cream

Metric	US	Imperial	
50g	½ stick	2oz	Butter
175g	⅓ cup	6oz	Rinded bacon, chopped
175g	⅓ cup	6oz	Parsley, finely chopped
			Salt and freshly ground black pepper
6	6	6	Eggs, large
100ml	⅓ cup	3fl oz	Whipping/heavy cream

Preheat the oven to 180°C/350°F/gas mark 4/FO 160°C.

Thickly butter 6 ramekins, about 150ml/½ cup/5fl oz capacity, and arrange them in a roasting tin.

Heat 2 tablespoons butter in a small frying pan and fry the bacon until lightly browned and crisp. Drain the bacon on kitchen paper, crush, then sprinkle on to the bases of the ramekins, adding the parsley and a little seasoning to taste. Break an egg into each dish.

Pour sufficient tap-hot water into the roasting tin to come halfway up the sides of the ramekins. Cover the tin with foil and bake for 16–18 minutes or until the whites of the eggs are set and the yolks are creamy.

Spoon some cream over each baked egg and serve immediately with fingers of buttered toast.

Tomato soufflé omelette

The nature of a plain omelette demands that the diner waits for it. With a soufflé omelette there is a double imperative: the cook needs to be organised from the moment the eggs are separated, in order that the billowing omelette can be put in front of the diner before there is even a suspicion of its decline.

Metric	US	Imperial	
			SAUCE:
15g	1 tbsp	½oz	Butter
15g	1 tbsp	½oz	Flour
325ml	1¼ cups	10fl oz	Whole milk
50g	½ cup	2oz	Mature Cheddar cheese, grated
1 tsp	1 tsp	1 tsp	Worcester sauce
			OMELETTE:
6	6	6	Eggs, separated
			Salt and freshly ground black pepper, to taste
25g	2 tbsp	1oz	Butter
3	3	3	Tomatoes, large, skinned, seeded and diced

Makes
Two large omelettes

Start by preparing the cheese sauce. Melt the butter in a small pan, stir in the flour and cook for a minute over a low heat before gradually adding the milk, stirring quickly to avoid the sauce forming lumps. Bring to the boil, then adjust the heat to give a gentle simmer and cook for 10 minutes.

Remove the pan from the heat and stir in the cheese and Worcester sauce, then season to taste. Put a circle of buttered greaseproof paper directly on top of the sauce and seal around the edges to prevent a skin forming. Keep warm.

Preheat the grill to slightly below its highest setting. Using an electric whisk, beat the egg yolks with two tablespoons of cold water. When they are light and frothy, wash the beaters thoroughly, dry and whisk the egg whites until they are stiff but not dry. Fold the yolks into the whites with a little seasoning.

Melt half the butter in a 20–5cm/8–9in omelette pan. Just as it starts to brown, pour in half the egg mixture. Cook over a moderate heat for a minute or two, then slip the pan under the grill just long enough for the mixture to puff and set golden on top.

Sprinkle with half the prepared tomatoes, fold in two and turn out on to a heated serving dish. Spoon over the hot cheese sauce and serve.

The omelettes can be made two at a time if you have two pans; if not, make one after the other.

Cheese and onions

Mature Cheshire cheese and raw onions, eaten with plain white bread, formed a regular supper in many North Country households. Hardly the most digestible of foods, they often produced dreams of quite memorable quality! In Lancashire, the cheese and onions were cooked; the following version, from Bolton-le-Moors, was eaten with currant-bread for supper on Sunday evenings. It is simple to make, and very tasty.

Metric	US	Imperial	
450g	1lb	1lb	Onions
325ml	1¼ cups	10fl oz	Whole milk
			Salt, to taste
50g	½ cup	2oz	Lancashire cheese, grated

Peel and quarter the onions and simmer in the milk and salt for around 25 minutes until tender. Drain off the milk (which can be used in soups), then stir the cheese into the cooked onions until it has all melted. Pour into warm bowls and serve with sliced currant-bread.

Cheese and tomato pudding

In the rush to eat a 'proper' diet of plenty of fresh fruit and vegetables we seem to have forgotten that raw tomatoes can be cooked. Here, they form a quick gratin-style recipe that can be served as a supper dish with a green salad, or to accompany a wide variety of roast, grilled and pan-fried meats or fish.

Metric	US	Imperial	
900g	2lb	2lb	Fresh tomatoes
50g	1 cup	2oz	White breadcrumbs made from stale bread
50g	½ cup	2oz	Parmesan cheese, grated
			Salt and pepper, to taste
25g	¼ stick	1oz	Butter

Preheat the oven to 190°C/375°F/gas mark 5/FO 170°C.
Butter a 1·8 litre/3pt gratin dish.

Slice tomatoes about 5mm/¼in thick, cutting away the central cores when you come across them. Lay half the sliced tomatoes in an even layer in the dish. In a bowl toss together the breadcrumbs, grated cheese and a generous amount of seasoning.

31

Sprinkle half this mixture over the tomatoes, cover with a final layer of tomatoes then the rest of the cheese/crumb mixture.

Put flecks of butter over the surface and then transfer to the oven to bake. Give it about 40 minutes, or until bubbling juices are clearly visible and the top is browned. Serve hot.

Cheese aigrettes

This is another recipe from Mrs Marshall. The dictionary interprets the French *aigrette* as either the crested head of a heron or the feathery seed head of a dandelion. These cheese puffs are *really* special.

Metric	US	Imperial	
25g	¼ stick	1oz	Butter
150ml	½ cup	5 fl oz	Water
50g	½ cup	2oz	Plain white flour
1	1	1	Egg
1	1	1	Egg yolk
85g	1 cup	3oz	Parmesan cheese, grated
			Salt, to taste
¼ tsp	¼ tsp	¼ tsp	Cayenne pepper
			Vegetable oil for frying

In a medium-sized, non-stick saucepan, combine the butter and the water and bring to the boil. Add the flour, all in one go, and beat until the mixture forms a thick paste around the spoon.

Remove the pan from the heat and continue beating until the pan has cooled to be just warm. At this stage beat in first the whole egg and yolk, then add the cheese. Season to taste, with salt and cayenne pepper. This mixture can be kept for up to two days if stored in a covered bowl in the fridge.

When ready to serve, heat a deep pan of oil to 180°C/350°F. Scoop teaspoons of the mixture into the oil and fry until golden brown. Remove with a draining spoon on to a baking tray lined with kitchen paper. Keep warm until all the mixture has been fried, then serve immediately.

Serve with a green salad and a piquant sauce if liked.

Opposite: Lanhydrock Dairy scullery showing the scalding range where pans of milk were heated by hot-water pipes to make clotted cream.
(*NTPL/Andreas von Einsiedel*)

Aiguilles of Parmesan

Great fun and delicious, but how and when should these crisp cheesy morsels be served? In the days when a 'starter' meant soup, these would probably have been used as a soup garnish. Nowadays, they would be better served at an informal drinks party, handing around portions in small greaseproof paper bags so people can eat them like an up-market packet of crisps. However you decide to serve them, you would be well advised to make double the quantity, as they are very moreish. For supper, with a big bowl of mixed green salad, they are wonderful.

Metric	US	Imperial	
150 ml	⅝ cup	5 fl oz	Whole milk
25 g	¼ stick	1 oz	Butter
50 g	⅔ cup	2 oz	Flour
2	2	2	Eggs, beaten
35 g	⅓ cup	1½ oz	Parmesan cheese, grated
¼ tsp	¼ tsp	¼ tsp	Cayenne pepper
			Salt
			Vegetable oil for deep frying
			Additional grated Parmesan cheese for serving

In a non-stick saucepan combine the milk and butter and bring to the boil. Add all the flour and beat until it forms a stiff paste around the spoon.

Remove the pan from heat and continue to beat until just warm. Now gradually beat in the eggs, then the cheese and cayenne, and season to taste with salt; the mixture should have a definite piquant flavour.

Heat a deep pan of oil to 180°C/350°F.

TAKE GREAT CARE WITH THE NEXT MANOEUVRE. Spoon the cheese mix into a metal colander and using a rubber spatula work the paste through the holes in the colander, so it drops directly into the pan of oil. It is best to fry half of the mixture at a time. Fry until golden brown, then scoop out with a large draining spoon on to a baking tray lined with kitchen paper.

Fry the rest of the mixture the same way and then turn out on to a baking tray. Sprinkle the aiguilles with additional Parmesan and serve with a mixed green salad.

Opposite: Jugged green pea soup (p.24).
(*Robin Weir/Andreas von Einsiedel*)

Cheese cutlets

A recipe adapted from that magnum opus *The Ideal Cookery Book* by M.A. Fairclough, 1911. This is a more homely version of the erstwhile bistro favourite – crumb-coated, deep-fried brie – and better, we think.

Metric	US	Imperial	
110g	1 cup	4oz	*Mature Cheddar cheese, grated*
25g	¼ stick	1oz	*Butter*
1 tsp	1 tsp	1 tsp	*English mustard powder*
			Salt and freshly ground black pepper
1	1	1	*Egg, beaten*
			A little flour for dusting
75g	1½ cups	3oz	*Dry white breadcrumbs*
4	4	4	*White bread slices, 5mm/¼in thick*
			Vegetable oil for frying

In a mixing bowl or food-processor, combine the cheese, butter, mustard powder and some seasoning. Add 1 tablespoon of beaten egg and beat together until the mixture forms a stiff paste. Transfer the cheese mix to a lightly floured board and divide into four equal portions. Pat each one into a neat lamb-chop/cutlet-type shape.

Dip each cutlet in the remaining beaten egg and then coat in breadcrumbs, pressing the crumbs on evenly and firmly with a small spatula.

Have a frying pan ready with sufficient oil to come half way up each side of the cutlets. Heat the oil over a moderately high heat and fry the cutlets on both sides until golden brown. Drain on kitchen paper and keep warm.

Using either a cutlet cutter or a sharp pointed knife, cut identical shaped cutlets from each slice of bread. Fry the bread shapes on both sides until golden brown. Drain on kitchen paper and cover each piece of fried bread with a cheese cutlet. Serve with a piquant chutney and a green side salad.

To fricassée a chicken

The origin of the word 'fricassée' is unknown. It was adopted in the sixteenth century from the French, who used it to describe mincing and cooking in sauce. In English cookery books it came to mean meat sliced, then fried or steamed and served with a sauce, as in this modified version of Mrs Raffald's recipe.

Metric	US	Imperial	
1·4 kg	3 lb	3 lb	Free-range chicken cut into 8 joints
125 ml	½ cup	4 fl oz	Dry white wine
½ tsp	½ tsp	½ tsp	Anchovy paste
3-4	3-4	3-4	Blades of mace
1	1	1	Small onion, peeled, left whole and stuck with 2 cloves
½	½	½	Lemon, cut in 4 chunks
			Marjoram, several sprigs
			SAUCE:
25 g	¼ stick	1 oz	Butter
25 g	2 tbsp	1 oz	Flour
2-3 tbsp	2-3 tbsp	2-3 tbsp	Whipping/heavy cream
			Salt and white pepper, to taste
			GARNISH:
2 tbsp	2 tbsp	2 tbsp	Chives, snipped
3-4 tbsp	3-4 tbsp	3-4 tbsp	Whipping/heavy cream

Rinse the chicken joints in cold water and put in a large pan with 1 litre/4 cups/35 fl oz water and all but the sauce ingredients. Heat until barely simmering; the gentler the cooking, the more tender the chicken. Cook in this manner, uncovered, for 30 minutes or until tender. Remove the joints with a draining spoon and keep covered on a plate.

Meanwhile, briskly boil the remaining contents of the pan until reduced to about 625 ml/2½ cups/20 fl oz – about 15 minutes. Strain the liquid, discard the flavouring ingredients and return the stock to the pan.

To make the sauce, work the butter and flour together to form a paste then whisk this into the stock, a little at a time. Bring to the boil, stirring. Add the cream and season to taste.

Return the chicken to the sauce, cover and reheat gently for 3-4 minutes or until well heated through.

Serve on a warmed dish, scatter with snipped chives and marble with a little fresh cream spooned all over.

Malay curry

To anyone accustomed to cooking curries this Edwardian recipe comes as quite a shock in its simplicity. Without the wide variety of spices to which we now have ready access, cooks had to make do with much less. Lady Clark's recipe produces a fairly mild chicken curry. For extra flavour, leave the chicken to marinate overnight in the stock and spices, then transfer to a pan and heat gently – and it should be gentle if the chicken is to become tender. You may find a heat-diffuser under the pan will help here.

Metric	US	Imperial	
50g	½ cup	2oz	Blanched almonds
1	1	1	Medium onion, peeled and coarsely cut
			Grated rind of 1 lemon
300 ml	1¼ cups	10 fl oz	Chicken stock
1 rounded tsp	1 rounded tsp	1 rounded tsp	Turmeric
½ tsp	½ tsp	½ tsp	Cayenne pepper
			Salt, to taste
1·7kg	3¾lb	3¾lb	Chicken cut into 6–8 joints
125 ml	½ cup	4 fl oz	Single/light cream
			Juice of ½ lemon

Brown the almonds either by grilling, baking in the oven or frying in a little vegetable oil. Put the almonds, onion and lemon rind in a spice-mill or food-processor with a little of the measured stock and liquidise to a paste. Transfer this to a sauté pan and stir in the turmeric and cayenne pepper, then the remaining stock and a little salt. Turn the chicken joints in the liquid, bring to just below simmering point, then cover and cook gently for about 30 minutes, turning the joints once or twice.

Uncover and cook for a further 15 minutes or until the chicken is completely tender.

Using a draining spoon, remove the chicken joints to a warmed serving dish, cover and keep warm.

Boil the remaining pan juices for 5 minutes to reduce the liquid and concentrate the flavour. Pour in the cream, and heat until bubbling. Remove the pan from the heat, add the lemon juice and season to taste. Pour over the chicken joints and serve. Good with pilau rice.

Mushroom-stuffed chicken with bread sauce

Metric	US	Imperial	
1·5 kg	3 lb 5 oz	3 lb 5 oz	Chicken
400 g	14 oz	14 oz	Button mushrooms
85 g	¾ stick	3 oz	Butter
½ tsp	½ tsp	½ tsp	Ground mace
¼ tsp	¼ tsp	¼ tsp	Cayenne pepper
			Salt
4	4	4	Streaky bacon, rinded and chopped
125 ml	½ cup	4 fl oz	Dry white wine
			BREAD SAUCE:
250 ml	1 cup	8 fl oz	Whole milk
25 g	¼ stick	1 oz	Butter
1	1	1	Onion peeled and quartered
3	3	3	Cloves
1	1	1	Bay leaf
50 g	1 cup	2 oz	Breadcrumbs
3 tbsp	3 tbsp	3 tbsp	Whipping/heavy cream

Heat the oven to 200°C/400°F/gas mark 6/FO 180°C. Have ready a roasting tin and rack on which to sit the chicken. Rinse the mushrooms in cold water and pat dry.

Heat the butter in a sauté pan until it just begins to brown. Stir in the mushrooms, spices and a sprinkling of salt and cook over a fairly high heat for about 5 minutes. Remove the pan from the heat and stir in the chopped bacon. Stuff this mixture and any pan juices into the body cavity of the bird, then either sew up or use skewers to close the opening and prevent the mushrooms falling out.

Pour the wine into the roasting tin, put the chicken on a roasting rack then transfer to the oven to cook for about 1½ hours, basting occasionally.

As soon as the chicken goes into the oven, combine the milk, butter, onion, cloves and bay leaf in a small saucepan, cover and leave over a very low heat for about 1 hour so that the mixture can infuse.

To check if the chicken is cooked, insert a thin skewer in the thickest part of the thigh; the juices should run golden and clear, not pink. Transfer the bird to a warmed serving plate and keep warm while finishing the bread sauce and making the gravy.

Strain the milk into a clean pan. Add the breadcrumbs and cream and reheat to a serving temperature. Season to taste and keep warm. Spoon off the excess fat from the roasting pan juices, reheat, season and serve with the chicken and bread sauce.

Devonshire chicken and parsley pie

A delicious pie, hot or cold. In fact, when cold the juices set to give a beautifully moist filling – ideal for a picnic. This recipe, adapted slightly, comes from the *Cook Book of Lady Clark of Tillypronie*, published in 1909; the original used chicken joints – on the bone. While our forebears were accustomed to negotiating bones in pies, our generation is not, and it is much easier to serve boneless.

Metric	US	Imperial	
1 tsp	1 tsp	1 tsp	*Nutmeg, freshly grated*
1 tsp	1 tsp	1 tsp	*Salt*
1 tsp	1 tsp	1 tsp	*Sugar*
			Black pepper, freshly ground, to taste
1·5 kg	3 lb 5 oz	3 lb 5 oz	*Chicken meat cut in 2·5 cm/1 in cubes*
20	20	20	*Finger-thick spring onions trimmed, leaving about 5 cm/2 in green*
2	2	2	*Shallots, peeled*
3 tbsp	3 tbsp	3 tbsp	*Parsley sprigs, rinsed and dried*
100 ml	6 tbsp	3½ fl oz	*Whipping/heavy cream*
			SHORTCRUST PASTRY:
300 g	2 cups	10 oz	*Plain flour*
150 g	1¼ stick	5 oz	*Butter*

Preheat the oven to 200°C/400°F/gas mark 6/FO 180°C. Put a heavy baking tray in the oven to heat.

In a large bowl combine the nutmeg, salt, sugar and a generous grinding of pepper. Toss the prepared chicken meat in this, cover and leave aside.

Finely chop the spring onions and shallots in a processor. Add the parsley and process again until everything is uniformly fine.

Cut the ball of made pastry in half and roll out into a circle that is big enough to line a round sloping-sided metal tart tin with a top measurement of 24 cm/9½ in, depth 4 cm/1½ in and a base measurement of 18 cm/7 in. Cut off any excess pastry that may be around the edge.

Sprinkle a third of the herb mix in the base of the pastry-lined tin to form an even layer. Now use one-third of the chicken to form a layer on top. Repeat the herb/chicken layers twice more. Shape the top of the filling to give a well-rounded, compact pie.

Roll out the remaining pastry and use to form a pie lid, binding the edges with a little milk. This pie produces gloriously flavoured juices which it is a shame to lose, so use a technique of folding the excess pastry of the lid under the rim of the side lining pastry. Then pinch together with thumb and forefinger for a good seal. Make a 2·5 cm/1 in diameter steam hole in the top of the pie. Transfer the pie tin to sit on the preheated baking tray in the oven. Bake for 15 minutes. Cover the pie with a buttered sheet of kitchen foil and continue baking for a further 15 minutes.

Now turn the oven temperature down to 180°C/350°F/gas mark 4/FO 160°C and bake for a further 40 minutes. Remove the foil and continue baking until the pastry is nicely browned and the filling is cooked; the best indication of this is when the juices start to bubble from the steam hole.

Remove the pie and leave to cool a little while you heat the cream to boiling point. If possible, use a small plastic funnel to pour the cream into the pie, via the steam hole. Have patience – it takes a little while for the cream to work its way into the pie.

Serve warm or cold. If serving warm, place the pie tin on a serving plate in case the juices overflow when it is cut.

Yorkshire pudding

Roast beef and Yorkshire pudding, served with good gravy, is perhaps the most quintessentially English dish. Everyone is familiar with the small bun-shaped Yorkshire puddings of café and restaurant catering, their weight and sogginess varying from one establishment to another. In their county of origin, however, they tend to be much larger, baked in large dripping pans to emerge with light, semi-crisp rolled edges, and thinner, but still light, centres, each person being given some of each as the pudding was cut into squares. Sometimes Yorkshire puddings were served as a separate course, with onion gravy, at the start of a meal, while others might be kept for serving as a sweet at the end. For sweet Yorkshire puddings, see p.58.

Metric	US	Imperial	
110g	¾ cup	4oz	Plain white flour
			Salt, to taste
2	2	2	Eggs
125ml	½ cup	4 fl oz	Whole milk
125ml	½ cup	4 fl oz	Water
1–2 tbsp	1–2 tbsp	1–2 tbsp	Beef dripping

Mix the flour and salt in a basin, and make a hole in the centre. Break in the eggs and gradually add the milk and water, beating the mixture continually to obtain a smooth batter. Leave it to stand for an hour. Put the dripping into a dripping pan, and preheat in the oven at 200°C/400°F/gas mark 6/FO 180°C until the fat is smoking hot. Pour in the batter, bake for 40 minutes until risen and brown.

Fish pie

This is one of those quiet army of recipes that forms the backbone of good, plain family cooking and goes marching on down the years. It is often a little despised because it is so ordinary – just poached fish in parsley sauce with mashed potato. For the cook there is an almost irresistible urge to throw modern ingredients at it. By all means substitute some of the fish with a packet of frozen mixed seafood, add some designer mushrooms, petit pois and vine-ripened tomatoes if it reassures you, but you will be losing the essential element of the dish, which is its undemanding, 'security blanket' simplicity.

Metric	US	Imperial	
700g	1½ lb	1½ lb	Cod or other white fish
550 ml	2¼ cups	18 fl oz	Whole milk
			Several blades of mace
			Salt and freshly ground black pepper
700g	1½ lb	1½ lb	Potatoes
50g	½ stick	2oz	Butter
3 tbsp	3 tbsp	3 tbsp	Plain white flour
1 tbsp	1 tbsp	1 tbsp	Anchovy essence
½ tbsp	½ tbsp	½ tbsp	or Patum Peperrium
3	3	3	Eggs, hard-boiled, peeled and chopped
250g	9oz	9oz	Prawns, cooked, shelled and halved (optional)
3 tbsp	3 tbsp	3 tbsp	Parsley
			Juice of ½ lemon

Preheat the oven to 200°C/400°F/gas mark 6/FO 180°C.
Butter a 1·8 litre/3pt baking dish.

Use a large pan to poach the fish fillets. Cut them in half and arrange in the base, then add the milk, mace and a little seasoning. Bring to simmering point and poach gently for about 5 minutes. Turn off the heat and leave to cool for several minutes before decanting the contents of the pan into a colander positioned over a large bowl.

As soon as the fish is cool enough to handle, separate into large flakes, removing the grey skin and discarding any bones and the mace. Reserve the fish and poaching liquid. Boil the potatoes in salted water until thoroughly cooked.

Meanwhile, melt the butter in a large pan and stir in the flour. Gradually add 400ml/14fl oz of the reserved poaching liquid to make a sauce. Bring to the boil and simmer gently for 5 minutes, then leave on one side.

Drain the boiled potatoes and return them to their pan with any remaining poaching liquid. Mash them, adding sufficient butter to form a soft creamy consistency. Season with some of the anchovy essence and pepper to taste.

Fold the fish into the sauce with the chopped eggs, prawns, if liked, and parsley. Season carefully with some additional anchovy essence and lemon juice. Spread the mixture into the baking dish, then gently spread the potato mixture over the surface.

Bake for about 20 minutes or until piping hot and browned on top.

Pan haggerty

An excellent Northumberland supper dish, with many regional variations. Among these are 'Pan ackelty', which is served with roast beef on top, and 'Pan jotheram', served with lamb chops on top.

Metric	US	Imperial	
25g	2 tbsp	1oz	*Butter, lard or bacon fat*
700g	1½lb	1½lb	*Potatoes, sliced (0·5cm/¼in thick)*
			Salt and freshly ground black pepper
1	1	1	*Spanish onion, peeled and very thinly sliced*
110g	1 cup	4oz	*Mature Cheddar cheese, grated*

You will need a large heavy frying pan, preferably with a fitted lid, although a fireproof plate would do instead.

Melt the fat in the pan and put in potato slices in an even layer. Season with salt and freshly ground black pepper before putting in the onions in a layer on top. Scatter with the grated cheese. Brush a large square of foil with a little oil and place this on top of the cheese, tucking it in up to the edge and leaving the excess foil to come up the side and bend over the rim of the pan. Bed the lid, or plate, firmly into the foil and leave to cook over a very low heat for 40 minutes without disturbing the pan. Preheat the grill.

Remove the lid and foil and transfer the pan to the grill. Once the cheese top has browned, remove and serve from the pan.

Smoked salmon tart

The smoking process is so mild nowadays that it produces smoked salmon that is moist to the point of plumpness, and with a very delicate flavour. This is far removed from Victorian versions where a far stronger salting and smoking meant the salmon had to be soaked before cooking. With this in mind, we tried this recipe using kipper fillets, a flavour more reminiscent of the original smoked salmon, and found it worked very well as a cheaper alternative.

Metric	US	Imperial	
			PASTRY:
225g	1²/₃ cup	8oz	*Plain white flour*
			Black pepper, freshly ground
110g	1 stick	4oz	*Butter*
1	1	1	*Egg yolk*
3 tbsp	3 tbsp	3 tbsp	*Cold water*
			FILLING:
225g	8oz	8oz	*Smoked salmon off cuts*
250ml	1 cup	½pt	*Whipping/heavy cream*
1	1	1	*Egg*
3	3	3	*Egg yolks*
			Salt and freshly ground black pepper
½ tsp	½ tsp	½ tsp	*Ground mace*

Combine the flour with a generous amount of freshly ground black pepper, then rub in the butter until the mixture resembles breadcrumbs. Combine the egg yolk and water, pour into the flour mixture and stir to combine. In the final stage use your hand to bring the mixture together to form a dough.

Roll out onto a lightly floured surface and use to line a buttered, fluted flan tin 25·5cm/10in diameter and 2·5cm/1in deep. Prick the base all over with a fork. If you have time, freeze the pastry-lined tin for 30 minutes as it helps the pastry keep a good shape when it bakes.

Preheat the oven to 200°C/400°F/gas mark 6/FO 180°C and put a heavy baking tray to heat in the oven.

Weight the pastry, lining it first with silicone paper, then filling evenly with baking beans. Transfer to the oven to bake on the baking tray for 15 minutes. Remove the beans and paper and return to the oven to bake for a further 5–10 minutes or until the pastry is cooked, but not coloured. Remove the tart tin from the oven and leave to cool, keeping the baking tray in the oven. Reduce the oven temperature to 190°C/375°F/gas mark 5/FO 160°C.

Arrange the salmon pieces evenly over the pastry base. Combine the egg, egg yolks, cream and a little seasoning and mace. Beat together with a balloon whisk until thoroughly mixed then pour over the salmon. Return the tart to the oven to cook on the baking tray for about 30 minutes. When it is set, lightly puffed in the centre and golden, remove from the oven and leave to cool. Best served warm.

Welsh eggs

A straightforward, unassuming recipe but a firm family favourite. Its origins are unknown but the Welsh connection is probably down to the leeks.

Metric	US	Imperial	
700g	1½lb	1½lb	*Floury potatoes, peeled*
1 tsp	1 tsp	1 tsp	*Salt*
6	6	6	*Leeks, trimmed*
50g	½ stick	2oz	*Butter*
6	6	6	*Eggs*
6 tbsp	6 tbsp	6 tbsp	*Whipping/heavy cream*
85–110g	3–4oz	3–4oz	*Strong Cheddar, grated*

Boil the potatoes in salted water. Drain and then either rub the potatoes through a coarse sieve or put through a potato ricer into a bowl.

Slice the leeks lengthwise, then across in approx. 1cm/½in strips. Wash thoroughly in cold water and drain well in a colander.

Melt the butter in a large pan, stir in the leeks, season, then cover and cook over a low heat. Add the sieved potatoes and mash together, seasoning if necessary.

Divide the mixture between 6 individual shallow, flameproof, buttered dishes. Cook the eggs in boiling water for 6 minutes then immediately plunge them into cold water to stop them cooking further. Switch on the grill so it has time to get hot whilst you carefully peel the eggs.

Make a hollow in the leek and potato mix, pour in a spoonful of cream and settle an egg in each hollow. Sprinkle generously with cheese then grill until melting and bubbling. Serve immediately.

Ramekins of smoked haddock and mushroom custard

This is a recipe given to us by our Publisher. Her mother used to make it as a supper dish when tempers were frayed or when stomachs still felt a little full after a lavish Sunday lunch.

She reports that it was handed down from her grandmother who came from Newcastle upon Tyne.

While her family makes the custard in one baking dish, with milk, we like it served in individual ramekins and made a little richer with cream. The former makes a good supper dish served with spinach and new potatoes; the latter makes an excellent starter with a dressed herb salad and melba toast.

Metric	US	Imperial	
225g	8oz	8oz	Skinned smoked haddock
1 tbsp	1 tbsp	1 tbsp	Butter
110g	4oz	4oz	Button mushrooms
600 ml	2½ cups	20 fl oz	Whole milk, or whole milk and cream mixed 50:50
2	2	2	Eggs
2	2	2	Egg yolks
3 tbsp	3 tbsp	3 tbsp	Chopped parsley
			Nutmeg, freshly grated
			Salt and freshly ground black pepper

Preheat the oven to 180°C/350°F/gas mark 4/FO 160°C.

Use a baking dish approx. 9½ × 6½in/24 × 16·5cm and approx. 900ml/1½pt capacity – or 6 individual ramekins. Butter the dish(es).

Cut the fish into bite-sized pieces. Heat the butter in a frying pan and fry the mushrooms briskly until they have given up their moisture and this has evaporated. Now add the fish and continue cooking for 2 minutes. Remove the pan from the heat and divide the mixture between the dishes. In the same pan heat the milk whilst you beat the eggs and egg yolks together in a bowl. When the milk is on the point of boiling pour it into the beaten eggs in a thin stream beating all the while. Add the parsley and nutmeg and season to taste before spooning the mixture over the fish. Put the dish(es) in a roasting tin and pour in sufficient warm water to come two thirds of the way up the side(s).

Cook for about 25 minutes for the ramekins, 35–40 minutes for the single dish, or until the custard has set in the centre and is tinged golden on top. The individual ramekins should be freed around the edges and turned onto salad lined plates.

Smoked trout with horseradish cream sauce

A very simple, unusual sauce, which is also good with poached fish and smoked chicken. Fresh horseradish is not readily available and something of a liability to grow, so you can substitute by using 4 tablespoons of hot horseradish sauce from a jar, in which case, you will not need the sugar.

Metric	US	Imperial	
150g	5oz	5oz	Fresh walnuts, shelled
2–3 tbsp	2–3 tbsp	2–3 tbsp	Fresh white breadcrumbs
2 tsp	2 tsp	2 tsp	Castor or ultra-fine sugar
300ml	1¼ cups	10 fl oz	Whipping/heavy cream
110–150g	4–5oz	4–5oz	Fresh horseradish, grated
4 tbsp	4 tbsp	4 tbsp	or horseradish sauce
2 tbsp	2 tbsp	2 tbsp	Cider vinegar
			Salt
6	6	6	Smoked trout fillets
			1 lemon, thinly sliced
2 tbsp	2 tbsp	2 tbsp	Small capers, drained

Pour boiling water over the walnuts and leave aside for 5 minutes. Peeling the walnuts will rid them of any bitterness, but the process of soaking them alone seems to help.

Put the walnuts in a blender with the remaining sauce ingredients and the lesser quantity of horseradish. Blend until reasonably smooth, then balance the flavour with additional sugar, vinegar, salt and horseradish as preferred. Serve with the trout fillets and some paper thin slices of lemon and chopped capers.

Chapter 3

CREAM PUDDINGS – HOT

Apple custard tart

Mrs Raffald calls for codlings in her version of this recipe in *The Experienced English Housekeeper*, 1769. Codlings, or quodlings as they were sometimes known, was a term used in the fifteenth and sixteenth centuries for under-ripe apples, and was the name for varieties of apple that were suitable only to be cooked. It seems that cooking apples, something peculiar to the English, are simply apples that remain unripened in our climate. Unripened apples always store better than the various types of eating apple. The best-known cooking apple, the Bramley, was named after Matthew Bramley, an English butcher, in whose garden at Southwell in Nottinghamshire this apple is said to have first grown in the early nineteenth century. The modern usage of the word codling is normally for an elongated apple, such as the Kentish Codling or the Keswick Codling.

This recipe will only work with cooking apples that will cook to a pulp.

Metric	US	Imperial	
900g	2lb	2lb	Cooking apples
175g	6oz	6oz	Puff pastry
100g	3/4 cup	3½oz	Raisins
4	4	4	Eggs
2	2	2	Egg yolks
50g	½ stick	2oz	Unsalted butter, softened
110g	½ cup	4oz	Castor or ultra-fine sugar
			Nutmeg, freshly grated
			DECORATION:
			Castor sugar

Preheat the oven to 220°C/425°F/gas mark 7/FO 200°C. Put a heavy baking tray in the oven to heat.

Quarter, peel and core the apples, then slice into a large pan. Add 1 tablespoon of water, cover and cook over a moderate heat, stirring frequently, until the apples have cooked to a pulp. Leave aside to cool.

Meanwhile, roll out the pastry thinly and line a round, sloping-side metal tart tin, base measurement 22cm/9in across, depth 4cm/1½in. Cut off the excess pastry around the edge and sprinkle the raisins in the base.

Beat the eggs, yolks, butter and sugar into the apple pulp until smooth – it should be rather like a pale custard. Taste and add more sugar if liked, and some grated nutmeg to taste.

Pour into the pastry-lined tin and put on the preheated baking tray in the oven. Reduce the heat to 180°C/350°F/gas mark 4/FO 160°C and bake for about 30 minutes or until well risen and browned on top.

Remove from the oven and leave to cool a little before serving. The filling will sink back to its original level but, dusted with some castor sugar and served with cream, it has an authentic look and is a good, well-flavoured tart.

"__ AY, HERE'S THE MASCULINE TO THE FEMININE GENDER."

_ Enter COWSLIP, with a bowl of Cream . _ Vide Brandenburg Theatricals.
"As a Cedar tall & slender ; __" Is her nom'tive case,
__ " Sweet Cowslips Grace __ " And she's of the feminine gender".

Malvern pudding

Another quiet little gem; apple pulp topped with sweetened egg sauce, finished with a burnt sugar topping. It sounds involved, and the ingredient list looks long, but it is very quickly made. Malvern pudding was probably invented when hasty pudding (a sweet sauce topped with sugar and spices) met with the apples of Worcestershire.

Metric	US	Imperial	
700g	1½lb	1½lb	Cooking apples
25g	¼ stick	1oz	Butter
2	2	2	Cloves
50g	¼ cup	2oz	Sugar, to taste
			SAUCE:
50g	½ stick	2oz	Butter
50g	⅓ cup	2oz	Plain/all-purpose flour
900ml	3¾ cups	30fl oz	Whole milk
50g	¼ cup	2oz	Sugar
3	3	3	Eggs, beaten
			TOPPING:
85g	¼ cup	3oz	Demerara sugar
¾ tsp	¾ tsp	¾ tsp	Ground mixed spice
15g	⅛ stick	½oz	Butter

Quarter, core and peel the apples, then slice into a large pan containing the hot melted butter. Add the cloves, cover with a lid and cook over a low heat for 12–15 minutes or until the apples have reduced to a pulp. Stir in the sugar, re-cover and remove the pan from the heat.

In a medium-sized pan, melt the butter for the sauce and stir in the flour. Stir the milk in gradually to form a smooth sauce. Boil gently for a minute or two then remove from the heat and stir in the sugar. Whisk the sauce as you gradually add the beaten eggs, then return the pan to a moderate heat. Cook, stirring, until the first bubble appears then remove the pan from the heat.

Remove the cloves and spread the hot apple pulp in the base of a 1·7 litre/7½ cup/3pt fireproof baking dish. Gently ladle the sauce on top, scatter with the combined demerara and mixed spice. Put the dish on a baking tray and toast the surface underneath a hot grill. Watch until the sugar caramelises, then remove immediately. Leave aside for about 10 minutes to allow the caramel to cool and become crisp. Serve hot or cold.

Queen of puddings, or Queen pudding

The earliest reference to this pudding, discovered by Jane Grigson was in Massey and Sons *Comprehensive Pudding Book* of 1875, where it is referred to as Queen Pudding. This book contains more than 1,000 puddings both sweet and savoury and 'the recipes are written clearly and concisely without the superfluity of words and tedious repetitions which characterise most culinary works'. In Masseys' book it was served cold, with apricot rather than blackcurrant or raspberry jam.

Metric	US	Imperial	
25g	¼ stick	1oz	*Butter*
110g	2 cups	4oz	*Fresh white breadcrumbs*
50g	¼ cup	2oz	*Castor or ultra-fine sugar*
2 tbsp	2 tbsp	2 tbsp	*Lemon rind, grated*
600ml	2¼ cups	18fl oz	*Whole milk*
2	2	2	*Eggs*
3 tbsp	3 tbsp	3 tbsp	*Blackcurrant or raspberry jam*

Preheat the oven to 180°C/350°F/gas mark 4/FO 160°C.

Use your fingers to butter thickly a 850ml/4 cup/1½pt pie dish. Put the remaining butter, breadcrumbs, half the sugar and the lemon rind in a bowl. Bring the milk to the boil and stir in the breadcrumb mixture.

Leave aside for 15 minutes to allow the bread to absorb some of the milk.

Now separate the eggs, beating the yolks into the cold breadcrumb mixture and putting the whites into a mixing bowl. Pour the breadcrumb mixture into a pie dish and bake for 30–35 minutes until set.

Meanwhile, warm the jam in a small pan. Pour it over the top of the set baked pudding and spread carefully to cover the surface.

Whisk the egg whites until they stand in soft peaks then gradually whisk in the remaining sugar. When the meringue is stiff spread it over the jam-topped pudding and give the surface several swirls before returning it to the oven.

Bake for a further 10–12 minutes or until the meringue is golden brown. Serve hot or warm.

Eliza Acton's 'good boiled' rice-pudding

This recipe can only be said to be 'loosely based' on Eliza Acton's recipe in *Modern Cookery*, published in 1845, as her method of cooking would seem to promise disaster. Whereas the rice mixture is cooked, below, in a bain-marie, Eliza Acton would have you cook this very liquid mix in a floured cloth. And not just cooked, but boiled. The result must have surely been a misshapen lump of sweet rice and scrambled egg.

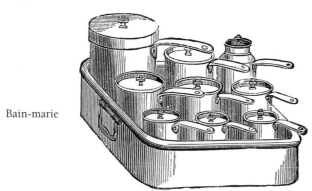

Bain-marie

Our method, given a more gentle cooking, produces a creamy, delicious dessert served, unusually these days, as a moulded pudding. We don't think you will hear the sound of Eliza turning in her grave.

Metric	US	Imperial	
125 g	½ cup	4 oz	Pudding rice
625 ml	2½ cups	20 fl oz	Whole milk
50 g	½ stick	2 oz	Butter
325 ml	1¼ cups	10 fl oz	Whipping/heavy cream
1	1	1	Vanilla pod
85 g	⅓ cup	3 oz	Castor or ultra-fine sugar
			Some butter for greasing
4	4	4	Eggs, large
			Grated rind of ½ lemon
¼ tsp	¼ tsp	¼ tsp	Bitter almond essence

Put the rice, milk, butter, cream and split vanilla pod in the top half of a double saucepan. Set over a base pan partly filled with cold water then leave over a low heat for about 1 hour, uncovered, stirring occasionally.

At this stage the rice should be soft and have absorbed the majority of the milk and cream. Stir in the sugar, remove the top half of the pan from the base and leave to cool for about 30 minutes. By this time there should be no free liquid left; if it is still a little milky leave for a further 15–30 minutes.

Preheat the oven to 160°C/325°F/gas mark 3/FO 140°C.

Use your fingers to butter thickly a 1·7 litre/7 cup/3pt heatproof bowl. Place the bowl in a roasting tin.

In a separate mixing bowl beat the eggs to a foam then stir in the lemon rind and bitter almond essence. Fold in the cooled rice, retrieving the vanilla pod. Use a tea-spoon to scrape the tiny vanilla seeds from inside the pod and return these to the rice mixture. The pod can be rinsed, dried and stored in sugar to make vanilla sugar.

Pour the rice into the buttered dish, then pour sufficient tap-hot water into the roasting tin to come about halfway up the side of the bowl; it is often easiest to do this once the roasting tin has been put in the oven. Cover the bowl with foil and leave to cook for about 1¾ hours or until the rice mixture is set in the centre. Remove from the oven and leave to cool.

When the pudding is at room temperature, run a knife around its edge to free the sides, then turn it out onto a plate and serve with poached fruit such as plums or rhubarb. It is also delicious with mixed dried fruits in port, or prunes cooked in claret.

A rich baked rice-pudding

The self-styled Dr Kitchiner, author of *The Cook's Oracle* first published in 1817, on whose recipe this baked rice-pudding is based, warns against the problems of adulterated milk in London. It was frequently thinned 'with sky blue [water] from the iron tailed cow [the pump]'. 'London Cream', we are told, is sometimes adulterated with milk thickened with potato-starch and tinged with turmeric; this explains why the Cockneys, on an expedition to the country, were so extremely surprised to find the thickest part of the cream at the top! Dr Kitchiner adds both cinnamon and nutmeg and suggests either baking it in puff pastry or boiling it in a floured cloth. We suggest that you bake it in a dish.

Metric	US	Imperial	
225g	1 cup	8oz	Pudding rice
1·7 litres	7½ cups	60fl oz	Whole milk
50g	¼ cup	2oz	Currants
50g	¼ cup	2oz	Raisins
50g	¼ cup	2oz	Castor or ultra-fine sugar
50g	½ stick	2oz	Butter
25g	1oz	1oz	Crystalised/candied orange
			Grated rind of 1 orange
1	1	1	Egg
3	3	3	Egg yolks
4 tbsp	4 tbsp	4 tbsp	Brandy

Put the rice in a large mixing bowl and pour in plenty of boiling water so the rice has enough room to expand. Leave aside for one hour and then drain and transfer to a deep baking dish.

Preheat the oven to 150°C/300°F/gas mark 2/FO 130°C. In a medium pan bring the milk to the boil before pouring over the drained rice. Stir in the dried fruit, sugar, butter, candied and grated orange rind. Beat together the egg, yolks and brandy, then stir this into the rice.

Place the baking dish in a large roasting tin and pour in enough tap-hot water almost to fill the tin. It is easiest to do this once the roasting tin has been put into the oven.

Bake for about 1½ hours or until the pudding is golden brown on top and softly set. Remove the baking dish from the water and serve the pudding warm or chilled. Whether hot or cold, it is good with a hot orange sauce or butter and brown sugar.

Dr Kitchiner's save-all pudding

Bread has been used traditionally as a thickener in both sweet and savoury dishes, and bread puddings have been made in England for many centuries. When encountering a pudding as robust as this, it is worth bearing in mind that the tradition of English puddings is based on the ready availability of milk and cream and the fact that people had larger appetites as a result of hard, physical work. Bread was much more substantial than it is today, so use ordinary, wholemeal bread, slightly stale, for this recipe, if possible.

This recipe from Dr Kitchiner's *Cook's Oracle* (1817) combines robust qualities with a rather frugal approach to cooking. Kitchiner was apparently not a man to waste anything. We have taken the liberty of introducing a touch of levity to this recipe by adding dried fruit.

Kitchiner was not a man to mince his words either. His dinner invitations were sent with a large red seal bearing the motto 'Better Never Than Late'. Invitations also clearly stated that dinner was at 5 o'clock, and when the first course was served, the front door was locked and no one else was admitted. There was a sign over the fireplace stating 'at eleven go'.

Metric	US	Imperial	
450g	1lb	1lb	Bread, brown or white slightly stale, sliced
600ml	2¼ cups	18 fl oz	Whole milk
115g	1 stick	4oz	Butter
400g	2¼ cups	14oz	Mixed dried fruit
85g	⅓ cup	3oz	Dark, soft brown sugar
4 tbsp	4 tbsp	4 tbsp	Chunky marmalade
3	3	3	Eggs
50g	⅓ cup	2oz	Plain flour
1 tsp	1 tsp	1 tsp	Baking powder
1 tbsp	1 tbsp	1 tbsp	Mixed spice
1 tsp	1 tsp	1 tsp	Ground cinnamon
¼	¼	¼	Nutmeg, freshly grated

Break the bread, including the crust, in pieces and put in a large mixing bowl. Pour the milk over the bread and leave aside while preparing the other ingredients. Thickly butter a roasting tin 30 × 24cm/12 × 9½in. Preheat the oven to 150°C/300°F/gas mark 2/FO 130°C.

Melt the butter in a small pan. Now beat the bread and milk mixture to a paste; it does not matter if it is slightly lumpy. Gradually stir in the rest of the ingredients in the order given in the recipe and finish by adding half the melted butter to the mixture.

Spread the mixture in the tin then pour the remaining butter over the surface. Bake for 2 hours, then raise the oven temperature to 180°C/350°F/gas mark 4/FO 160°C to give the pudding a crunchy crust.

Remove from the oven and leave to cool in the tin. Scatter with a little granulated sugar and serve warm or chilled, cut in squares with real custard.

White pot, or Rich bread and butter pudding

The combination of bread, milk and eggs are endless and varied in the history of English puddings. This is an example of the reconstructed style, where slices of bread and butter are layered with dried fruits in a baking dish. The liquid element is poured on and the pudding left aside to allow the bread to absorb the maximum before baking. A deconstructed style of pudding is bread pudding à la Dr Kitchiner – save-all pudding – (p.53) where all the ingredients are mixed together and baked. For a minimalist version you will find recipes with titles such as 'Poor Man's Pudding', 'Pain Perdu' or 'Poor Knights of Windsor', consisting of single slices of bread dipped in sweetened milk and beaten egg, then fried in butter.

Variations of bread and butter pudding include the addition of more exotic fruits, such as apricots and cherries, and more cream, spices, sherry or brandy. The bread can be spread with marmalade or lemon curd and the whole sweetened with honey and sugar. As an example of just how far variations can be pushed, Mary Norwak in *English Puddings* quotes Prince Charles's favourite bread and butter pudding as a combination of black treacle, banana and brandy.

Note: Any traditional style of bread-based pudding is improved by using traditionally baked bread rather than the modern supermarket sliced loaf.

Metric	US	Imperial	
25–50g	¼–½ stick	1–2oz	*Butter at room temperature*
8–10	8–10	8–10	*White bread, thin slices*
50g	¼ cup	2oz	*Currants*
25g	⅛ cup	1oz	*Mixed, chopped peel*
			Finely grated rind of 1 lemon
250ml	1 cup	8fl oz	*Whole milk*
125ml	½ cup	4fl oz	*Whipping/heavy cream*
3	3	3	*Eggs*
50g	¼ cup	2oz	*Castor or ultra-fine sugar*
			Nutmeg, freshly grated

Preheat the oven to 150°C/300°F/gas mark 2/FO 130°C.

Use your fingers to butter thickly a gratin baking dish, 1·2 litre/5 cup/2pt capacity. Butter the bread slices. Some people prefer to remove the bread crusts, but as long as the bread pudding is soaked before cooking it is not necessary.

Halve the bread slices and arrange in layers with currants, peel and lemon rind in between. Beat together the milk, cream, eggs and sugar, together with a good grating of nutmeg. Pour the mixture over the pudding and leave aside for one hour before baking.

Bake the pudding uncovered in the top half of the oven for about 2 hours then raise the heat to 180°C/350°F/gas mark 4/FO 160°C and cook for about 30 minutes until the top is crispy.

Welsh buttermilk griddle pancakes

Metric	US	Imperial	
175g	1¼ cup	6oz	Plain white flour
40g	¼ cup	1½oz	Castor or ultra-fine sugar
¼ tsp	¼ tsp	¼ tsp	Salt
3	3	3	Eggs
3 tbsp	3 tbsp	3 tbsp	Whipping/heavy cream
4 tbsp	4 tbsp	4 tbsp	Water
½ tsp	½ tsp	½ tsp	Bicarbonate of soda
½ tbsp	½ tbsp	½ tbsp	Cream of tartar
125 ml	½ cup	4 fl oz	Buttermilk or soured milk

Combine the flour, sugar and salt in a large bowl. Make a well in the centre and break in the eggs, then spoon in the cream. Since the cream of tartar and bicarbonate of soda start to react as soon as they are mixed with water, pause at this stage to heat the griddle on the stove top at a setting just below moderate. Pour the mixed raising agents and water into the bowl and start to beat the liquid ingredients with a balloon whisk. Gradually incorporate the surrounding flour and continue beating until all the flour has been combined to form a smooth batter. Now slowly add the buttermilk or soured milk until the right consistency is reached.

Lightly grease the griddle, then use a ladle to scoop batter from the bowl and pour in small puddles onto the griddle. Once bubbles have appeared and the surface of the pancakes is still liquid but manageable, free each one from the surface with a thin palette knife. Flip the pancakes over and cook briefly on the other side.

As they cook, remove the pancakes, spread with butter, and drizzle with honey and stack on top of each other. This keeps the pancakes warm and allows the butter and honey to permeate. Serve warm.

Elderflower fritters with muscat syllabub

This versatile, simple, super-crisp batter can be adapted to suit the food it is to coat – use a beer batter to coat vegetables and fish, cider for apples, a sweet, aromatic wine for strawberries and elderflowers. For sweet dishes the syllabub can be similarly adapted, again using cider or apple juice with apple fritters, a muscat wine or elderflower cordial with elderflower fritters, and, for a gourmet treat, add framboise or kirsch to a syllabub to serve with strawberries or other fruits.

Note: Make sure the elderflowers you pick are fragrant varieties from a garden uncontaminated by garden sprays, and away from roadside pollution.

Metric	US	Imperial	
			SYLLABUB:
4 tbsp	4 tbsp	4 tbsp	*Frontignan or similar dessert wine*
1 tbsp	1 tbsp	1 tbsp	*Lemon juice*
25g	2 tbsp	1oz	*Castor or ultra-fine sugar*
125 ml	½ cup	4 fl oz	*Whipping/heavy cream*
			BATTER:
100g	¾ cup	3½ oz	*Plain white flour*
25g	2 tbsp	1oz	*Cornflour*
375 ml	1½ cups	12 fl oz	*Dry white wine, pale ale, or skimmed milk*
			About 12 elderflower heads, clean and dry
			Oil for deep frying
			Icing sugar for dusting

Make the syllabub first, so it has some time to chill before serving.

Combine the wine, lemon juice and sugar together in a mixing bowl and leave aside for a short while, stirring occasionally until the sugar has dissolved. Gradually whisk in the cream and continue beating until the cream is stiff enough to hold a shape. Cover and chill in the fridge for about 2 hours.

Start to heat a pan of deep oil to 375°F/190°C.

For speed, combine the batter ingredients in a food-processor and blend. Otherwise, sift the flours into a mixing bowl. Make a well in the centre and use a balloon whisk gradually to incorporate the flour and wine, ale or milk into a smooth batter. If it is not smooth, simply pour through a sieve to take out the lumps.

One at a time, take the clean, dry flower heads by the stalk end and dip in the batter. Gently knock off the excess batter, then fry in the deep oil until golden brown. Remove with a draining spoon and put on absorbent paper, then transfer to a serving plate and keep warm in the oven until sufficient have been fried for one serving all round. Serve piping hot, dusted with icing sugar, accompanied by the chilled syllabub.

Ratafia custard tart

This recipe is loosely based on one in the *Cook Book of Lady Clark of Tillypronie* (1909). It is a twist on the classic egg custard tart, with an added almond flavour that comes through best when it is served warm.

If you are unable to get ratafia biscuits, use boudoir biscuits and add a little more almond extract. If you want an even more luscious consistency, some cream can be substituted for the milk. Jane Grigson writing in *English Food* says that this type of tart, called a 'doucet', was served as part of the third course at Henry IV's coronation banquet in 1399.

Metric	US	Imperial	
			FILLING:
			Shortcrust pastry to line tart tin
1 litre	4 cups	32 fl oz	*Whole milk*
4	4	4	*Eggs*
2	2	2	*Egg yolks*
85g	¾ stick	3oz	*Butter*
3 tbsp	3 tbsp	3 tbsp	*Sugar*
110g	4oz	4oz	*Ratafia biscuits, coarsely crumbled*
50g	2oz	2oz	*Boudoir biscuits (sponge fingers), coarsely crumbled*
50g	⅔ cup	2oz	*Blanched almonds, finely ground*
½ tsp	½ tsp	½ tsp	*Bitter almond extract*

Preheat the oven to 200°C/400°F/gas mark 6/FO 180°C.

Put a heavy baking tray in the oven to heat. Lightly butter a round sloping-sided tart tin with a top measurement of 29cm/11½in and a depth of 4cm/1½in deep. Line with shortcrust pastry, then prick the base all over with a fork. Transfer to the oven to bake on the baking tray for 10-15 minutes, where it will cook slightly. Remove the tart from the oven, leaving the baking tray in the oven.

Reduce the oven temperature to 160°C/325°F/gas mark 3/FO 140°C.

While the pastry cools, bring the milk to the boil, beat the eggs and yolks together in a mixing bowl. When the milk rises in the pan, steadily pour it into the eggs, whisking all the while. Add the remaining ingredients, whisking to dissolve the butter, sugar and biscuits. Taste for sweetness and leave to cool. When the egg mixture is cool pour it carefully into the pastry-lined tart tin and place the tin on the baking tray in the oven. Leave to bake for 1-1¼ hours. When ready, the filling will be gently set, lightly puffed around the edge and pale golden. Serve warm.

Note: Bitter almond extract is available from Culpepper (see useful addresses p.140).

Sweet Yorkshire pudding

We have repeated the recipe for Yorkshire puddings here, but this time they have a sweet filling for serving as hot desserts.

Metric	US	Imperial	
110g	¾ cup	4oz	Flour, plain
			Salt, to taste
2	2	2	Eggs
125ml	½ cup	4fl oz	Whole milk
125ml	½ cup	4fl oz	Water
1-2 tbsp	1-2 tbsp	1-2 tbsp	Beef dripping

Mix the flour and salt in a basin, and make a hole in the centre. Break in the eggs and gradually add the milk and water, beating the mixture continually to obtain a smooth batter. Leave it to stand for an hour. Put the dripping into a dripping pan, and preheat in the oven at 200°C/400°F/gas mark 6/FO 180°C until the fat is smoking hot. Pour in the batter, bake for 40 minutes until risen and brown.

This can be served as a sweet pudding by spreading it with any of the following:

- *Golden syrup or maple syrup.*
- *Raspberry jam.*
- *Raspberry jam mixed with malt vinegar, to give a 'sweet and sour' taste.*
- *Raspberry vinegar.*
- *Butter and sugar.*

Alternatively, the following may be mixed into the batter:

- *A large baking apple, peeled and grated.*
- *A large baking apple, peeled, sliced and spread over the batter when it has just been poured into the dripping pan.*
- *1 or 2 sticks of forced rhubarb cut in short pieces and mixed in. This is usually served with a sweet white sauce.*

Thin pancakes with hard sauce

Hard sauce would seem to be something of an oxymoron to anyone who is not accustomed to Christmas pudding with rum or brandy butter; the flavoured butter is an example of a hard sauce.

Metric	US	Imperial	
			HARD SAUCE:
110g	1 stick	4oz	Unsalted butter
110g	½ cup	4oz	Castor or ultra-fine sugar
			Finely grated rind of 1 lemon
1 tbsp	1 tbsp	1 tbsp	Boiling water
1 tsp	1 tsp	1 tsp	Lemon juice
4 tbsp	4 tbsp	4 tbsp	Cream sherry
			PANCAKES:
250 ml	1 cup	8 fl oz	Single/light cream
100g	¾ cup	3½oz	Plain white flour
2	2	2	Eggs
2	2	2	Egg yolks
25g	2 tbsp	1oz	Castor or ultra-fine sugar
1 tbsp	1 tbsp	1 tbsp	Cream sherry
			Nutmeg, freshly ground
1 tbsp	1 tbsp	1 tbsp	Butter, melted
			TO SERVE:
			Some additional castor or ultra-fine sugar
			A little icing sugar

To make the hard sauce, put the butter, sugar and lemon rind in a bowl. Beat until creamy and light, then beat in the boiling water. Now beat in the lemon juice and sherry. Cover and keep in the fridge until ready to serve. If the fridge temperature is correct (about 4°C/39°F), it will keep for about three weeks.

Make the batter either by blending all the pancake ingredients in a processor, or by putting the flour and cream in a mixing bowl and, using a balloon whisk, blending to a smooth batter before adding the remaining ingredients. Use a standard, iron pancake pan. This only needs to be greased to make the first pancake; the melted butter in the batter makes the pancakes self-basting. With this quantity you should be able to make at least 8 pancakes.

Cook the pancakes on both sides over a slightly below moderate heat; this will take a maximum of 1½ minutes for both sides.

Turn the pancakes out to form a stack, dotting with a little butter and sprinkling with a little sugar between each layer. Dust the top pancake with icing sugar and serve immediately cut in wedges, handing round the hard sauce.

Chapter 4
CREAM PUDDINGS – COLD

There are very few dishes which, for sheer cool succulence and delicacy of flavour, can match the creamy delights of English country-house cookery. Although often made by French chefs, they really form part of the traditional housekeeper's repertoire, exemplified in the works of Mrs Raffald, Mrs Glasse and their Georgian contemporaries. All the cooking facilities they needed were available in the still-rooms and kitchens, but for these dishes in particular it was essential to have access to the dairy. This was neither the farm dairy nor the pleasure-ground dairy, but the dairy pantry, situated in the service wing of the main house, amid the other pantries and larders.

Into this pantry fresh supplies of all manner of dairy products arrived each day delivered by donkey, cart or milk boy. At Penrhyn in North Wales, the milk boy used a yoke to carry two four-gallon cans, each with a smaller cream-can hanging on its handle, as well as a basket of eggs and another of butter, from the home farm, up to the castle each morning before 8am. Once checked into the castle dairy pantry, the order was given for the afternoon supplies, and then the milk was carried to the rooms of the housekeepers, housemaids and footmen, where it was poured into jugs ready for their use.

The internal dairy pantries were usually fitted out with tiled walls, slate or marble wall-benches and tables, smooth stone, slate or tiled floors, and provided with a water supply and drainage so that they could be easily swilled down. Fresh air was provided by gauze-covered window panels or ventilation ducts, while in the finer examples, such as Dyrham Park in Gloucestershire, a tall fountain played water into a deep round bowl, keeping the atmosphere cool and moist. This was the ideal place in which to store raw milk, butter, cream and covered cheeses ready for the kitchen or table, as well as the junkets, blancmanges, custards and jellies made by the cook or the housekeeper.

Most of these cold cream puddings have a surprisingly long history, going back to at least the early medieval period. They all have one distinct characteristic: they are simply milk or cream made thick enough to eat with a spoon. Only the method by which this was achieved changed, and it is interesting to follow these developments through the centuries.

The custard, for example, started life as a *crustade*, from the Latin *crusta* for a hard rind or shell. It was an open tart of meat, fish or herbs, often bound with eggs like a modern quiche. By around 1600 it had lost its savoury fillings, becoming a sweet baked custard. Its batter of cream, eggs and sugar flavoured with mace or ginger, or almond milk and rose water, was ladled into fantastically shaped pie-crusts, already half-baked on the floor of stone ovens. By the eighteenth century, plainer custards were being baked in most kitchens. In Whitby in York-shire, they were always eaten on Easter Sunday, the cold easterly winds hitting the coast at this season being locally known as 'custard winds'.

Liquid custards, made by stirring the ingredients over a gentle heat until they could coat the back of a spoon, but certainly not simmered to form a curd, were popular as a sauce for puddings and to coat those brandy-soaked columns of firm sponge called tipsy cakes, effectively sealing in all their alcohol. They form the basis of most ice creams too. But, at their best, their uncooked batter, flavoured with almonds, cinnamon and orange flower water, or Seville orange juice, rind and brandy, was poured into glass custard-cups standing in a pottery bowl of hot water within the oven, and allowed to set. These delicacies were ideal for Georgian and Victorian dinners and ball suppers.

In Tudor and Stuart England there was virtually no difference between a baked custard and a fool. Randle Holme in his *Academy of Armoury*, published in 1688, described a fool as 'a kind of Custard, but more crudely, being made of Cream, Yolk of Eggs, Cinamon, Mace boiled; and served on sippets [thin slices of bread] with sliced Dates, Sugar, and white and red Comfits strawed theron.' A dish we might call a fool had been known as 'apple moise', or 'apple moyl' in the fourteenth and fifteenth centuries, this being a smooth purée of cooked apples thickened with a variety of ingredients, including egg yolks. It was not until the Georgian period, however, that fools achieved their modern form, in which the sharp flavours of fruit purées ideally enhance the rich smooth creaminess of their custard bases.

Another way to thicken and flavour cream and milk was to add a natural acidity of some kind, so as to convert it into a fine soft curd. Perhaps the oldest method was to lay a cured strip of a calf's inner stomach into a bowl of milk at blood heat. Orig-inally the curd might then have been drained in a mat or basket of rushes, called in old Norman French a *jonquet*, from 'jonc' the word for rushes, to form a firm junket. The Victorians produced essence of junket, which gave identical results with a much greater degree of convenience. But around 1900 the old ways were still being followed in Devon and Cornwall. Every May Day at midnight in Penzance, crowds of young people set off from the inns with music bands to visit local farm-houses, there to 'partake of a beverage called junket, made of raw milk and rennet, sweetened with sugar, and a little cream added, followed by heavy cake and rum and milk'. The following Sunday they set off once more to local farm dairies 'where young ones find delicious junkets … which is eaten with sugar and cream'.

The addition of wine to milk and cream produces similar results, called syllabub. Perhaps the earliest method, practised by the Tudors and Stuarts, was to hold a bowl of cider, wine or verjuice under the cow's udder, and squirt the milk into it with some pressure. The resulting unappetising curd was then removed, and the whey beaten up with cream, wine and sugar. Alternatively, these ingredients could be beaten together first, and the bowl then set beneath the cow. For those who could not readily find a convenient cow, syringes called 'wooden cows', or even jugs or teapots could be used as substitutes. This sort of syllabub was poured into small cylindrical glasses or earthenware pots with handles on the sides, and a swan-necked spout at the front. Here it separated, so that the firm creamy curd above could be eaten with a spoon, and the alcoholic whey below sucked from the spout.

From the seventeenth century, whipped syllabubs were made by beating mixtures of cream, wine and sugar with whisks made of birch rods, willow twigs or rotating chocolate mills. This gave an amazingly light foam, which was skimmed off as it arose, and built up, layer on layer, in a sieve, where it remained for perhaps a day to form a rather firmer foam; this could be spooned into the broad tops of special syllabub glasses, already half filled with red or white wine.

If lemon juice was beaten into cream, along with white wine and sugar, it formed quite a firm curd. From the mid-eighteenth century this was poured into muslin-lined, cream-ware moulds, rather like jelly moulds, but perforated with a pattern of small punched holes. Allowing twelve hours or more for the whey to drain away, the curd was solid enough to be turned out on to a plate, and the muslin removed to reveal an Italian cream of particular richness.

Tin moulds

The most usual method of making cream and milk moulds, however, was by using gelatine. This used to be a rather exclusive ingredient, since it took days to boil the calf's feet and then clarify and reduce the stock to form a firm jelly. There were further problems too, since boiling gelatine and cream or milk together produces a rather unpalatable curdled mass. Elizabethan cooks overcame these problems quite admirably to produce two distinct sweets. One was called 'leach', a word meaning slice, and certainly not referring to any ingredient. This was a firm cream and rose water jelly, which melted in the mouth like the coolest, most delicate and non-cloying Turkish Delight. The Tudors served this in chunks coated in gold-leaf at their finest banquets. The other milk/cream jelly was called 'blancmange', meaning 'white food'. By the 1590s it had been transformed from a compounded mass of ground chicken with rice, sugar and almond milk, to a lighter sweeter jelly with added rice-flour, rose water and almonds. Over the following years various blancmanges were made with similar ingredients; only the introduction of arrowroot, and later in the Victorian period, cornflour, brought it to the comparatively tasteless 'shape' of pre-war institutional cookery.

As the following recipes show, our traditional cold cream desserts can still provide the most delicious end to any luncheon, tea or dinner.

Junket

The range of possibilities for flavoured junkets is vast. However, they are at their best with simple delicate flavours. Junkets are unbelievably simple to make, and provided you stick to a few simple rules you will have a success every time. Care and accuracy are all that is needed.

Rennet in Britain is supplied in liquid form in bottles (see useful addresses on p.140). It has a fairly short shelf life and an opened bottle of junket does not last for more than a few weeks. In the USA it is supplied in tablets (see useful addresses p.140), which make a sweeter junket and last much longer. You need an accurate thermometer and a cool place to store the junket once it is made. On no account should a junket be moved at all for the first 10 minutes while it is solidifying.

You must use full cream milk; long-life, canned, skimmed, semi-skimmed or any other sort of treated milk will not set properly. If you are on a diet, make a junket and share it with your friends so that you eat only a small amount.

Plain vanilla junket

Metric	US	Imperial	
625 ml	2½ cups	20 fl oz	Whole milk
3 tbsp	3 tbsp	3 tbsp	Sugar
1 tsp	1 tsp	1 tsp	Vanilla extract (not essence)
-	1	-	Junket tablets (US)
-	1 tbsp	-	Water (US)
1 tbsp	-	1 tbsp	Rennet (UK)

Have ready a 750ml/3 cup/1½pt bowl or a shallow junket bowl or several small dishes in which to serve the junket.

Warm the milk to 37°C/99°F with the sugar and stir to make sure it has dissolved completely, then add the vanilla and taste to check its strength.

WITH RENNET, put the warmed milk into a bowl and add 1 tablespoonful of rennet, stirring for no more than 3-5 seconds as it starts to set immediately. Do not move the bowl for at least 10 minutes. Store somewhere cool until you are ready to serve, preferably not in a fridge, which makes the junket tough.

WITH JUNKET TABLETS, crush the tablet in a bowl with 1 tablespoonful of water. Add this to the sweetened warmed milk stirring for no more than 3-5 seconds, as it starts to set immediately. Do not move the bowl for at least 10 minutes. Store somewhere cool until you are ready to serve, preferably not in a fridge, which makes the junket tough.

Variations

For a creamier junket you can add up to 50 per cent single/light cream.

Serve with whipping/heavy cream floated on the top or, for a real treat, serve with Cornish clotted cream.

Saffron junket

Saffron gives junket a wonderful colour and flavour. Add to the junket a packet of saffron powder (130mg) or a pinch of saffron. If you are using strands, put through a sieve to remove the strands before adding the rennet. Taste carefully as the quality of saffron varies enormously.

Rose water *or* Orange flower water junket

Substitute two tablespoons of rose water or orange flower water for 2 tablespoons of milk and make exactly as above. You must use a really good quality rose or orange flower water (see useful addresses p.140). Serve with cream floated on the top and decorate with rose petals.

Opposite: Rose water junket.
(*Robin Weir/Andreas von Einsiedel*)

Blancmange

He coude rost, and seethe and broil and frye,
Make mortreux [hash or stew], and well bake a pie …
… For blankmanger, that made he with the beste.

The Cook in the Prologue to Chaucer's *Canterbury Tales* certainly had a reputation as a blancmange maker, even though on the journey to Canterbury he was too drunk to complete his tale to the other travellers and fell off his horse!

Blancmange was originally a savoury moulded food that contained chicken and sometimes fish. It was often made with almond milk (p.77) and isinglass (obtained from the air bladders of some freshwater fish), but the latter is really too difficult to find anymore, and is available only from wine-makers' suppliers. The characteristics of the various basic ingredients make the blancmanges quite different. We prefer the cornflour-based one to gelatine, which produces a more bouncy and watery finish, while the arrowroot version is much more difficult to make.

If you wish to make blancmanges in old fashioned or antique moulds, avoid using copper moulds which are not tinned on the inside. It is best to oil them, using a tasteless oil (almond oil is ideal), before the hot blancmange is poured in.

If you are using a mould with a capacity of more than 600 ml/2½ cups/20 fl oz, it will not be possible to get a blancmange that will turn out successfully using only two tablespoons of cornflour per recipe. We suggest increasing the amount of cornflour to three tablespoons per recipe to give a mixture strong enough to hold its shape when turned out of the mould.

In addition you should use either a double saucepan, or a glass bowl over a saucepan of boiling water to avoid the thicker mixture catching on the bottom. Make sure that it is smooth and cooked thoroughly.

When you are ready to turn it out of the mould, free the blancmange around the edges by rotating it at an angle and letting some air get down the sides of the blancmange. This will release the air lock. As with jellies, turn out onto a wet plate so if it is not in the centre, it can be moved slightly.

If you are planning to make a large blancmange in a mould for a party, make sure that you try it out in advance!

Opposite: Everlasting syllabub (p.73).
(*Robin Weir/Andreas von Einsiedel*)

Gelatine blancmange

Gelatine, produced from the skin and bones of animals, is ideal for setting milk and cream because it has neither taste nor smell providing it is properly refined.

Metric	US	Imperial	
625 ml	2½ cups	20 fl oz	*Whole milk*
3 tbsp	3 tbsp	3 tbsp	*Sugar*
1½ tbsp	1½ tbsp	1½ tbsp	*Gelatine, granulated*
4 leaves	4 leaves	4 leaves	*or leaf gelatine*

Put the milk and sugar in a saucepan and raise to boiling point. Allow to cool for 2–3 minutes and then sprinkle the granulated or leaf gelatine slowly on to the milk, stirring constantly to ensure that it completely dissolves. On no account let the gelatine boil or it will separate. For flavouring, see p.68.

Cornflour blancmange

Cornflour is finely ground maize flour. The exact grinding process was discovered in the mid-nineteenth century and used extensively in both Britain and North America as a thickener and pudding-maker. Mid-Victorian recipes often refer to Patent Cornflour, as many manufacturers sought patents on the grinding process.

Metric	US	Imperial	
2 tbsp	2 tbsp	2 tbsp	*Cornflour*
625 ml	2½ cups	20 fl oz	*Whole milk*
3 tbsp	3 tbsp	3 tbsp	*Sugar*

Put the cornflour into a 1 litre/2pt bowl and mix it until smooth with about one-quarter of the milk. Heat the rest of the milk with the sugar to boiling point and then, stirring all the time, quickly pour the boiling milk into the cornflour mix. Stir until smooth and return the mixture to the pan taking care that it does not catch on the base. With a heat diffuser under the pan, reheat the mixture to boiling point and simmer for 3–4 minutes, stirring frequently, until cooked and thickened. For flavouring, see p.68.

For a firmer blancmange, use an additional half or whole tablespoon of cornflour.

Arrowroot blancmange

Arrowroot has an interesting taste all of its own but is rarely used for blancmanges nowadays. It produces a rather slippery consistency and is quite difficult to turn out, as it is nowhere near as firm as a cornflour or gelatine blancmange. The arrowroot also takes longer to thicken than cornflour, so it is essential to use a double saucepan to prevent it catching on the bottom of the pan.

Metric	US	Imperial	
3 tbsp	3 tbsp	3 tbsp	*Arrowroot powder*
625 ml	2½ cups	20 fl oz	*Whole milk*
3 tbsp	3 tbsp	3 tbsp	*Sugar*

Put the arrowroot into a 1 litre/2 pt bowl and mix with about one-quarter of the milk until smooth. Make sure that it is completely mixed before proceeding. Heat the rest of the milk with the sugar to boiling point and then, stirring all the time, quickly pour the boiling milk into the arrowroot mix. Stir until smooth and then return the mixture to a double saucepan, making sure that the water does not touch the bottom of the upper pan. Cook with the water simmering for 30 minutes, stirring every 5–10 minutes. It will thicken considerably during this time. Taste to ensure that there is no powder flavour and that it is completely cooked. For flavouring, see p.68.

Flavouring Blancmanges

You should always subtract an equivalent volume of milk to that of the flavouring you use. You can substitute up to 50 per cent single/light cream for milk to make a richer blancmange.

Bay leaf blancmange

Put two bay leaves in the milk and leave to infuse overnight. Heat with the milk mixture and remove before allowing to set.

Rose water *or* Orange flower water blancmange

Make any one of the basic blancmange recipes, as above, but remove 3 tablespoons of milk from the mixture. When thickened and cooling, add 2 tablespoons of flower water to the blancmange, stir carefully and taste. Add another tablespoon if liked, but remember that the flavour should be delicate.

We always bring back rose and orange flower water from the Santa Maria Novella pharmacy in Florence, as the quality is superior to any other we have found. However, it is now available in London and New York (see useful addresses p.140).

Quince blancmange

To make quince blancmange you need quince juice. This can be made when quinces are available and then frozen in small containers and used when required. Buy quinces and allow them to ripen – the smell of ripening quinces is reason enough to buy them. However, if they have no perfume, you will almost certainly be disappointed. Our experience is that the more miserable the quince looks, the better the flavour.

To make quince juice:

Metric	US	Imperial	
1·25 litres	5 cups	40 fl oz	*Water*
350g	1¾ cups	12 oz	*Sugar*
1–1·5 kg	2½–3 lb	2½–3 lb	*Quinces*
Makes about			
1·6 litres	6½ cups	2½ pints	

Put the water and the sugar in a non-reactive saucepan (i.e. not aluminium, unless coated). Peel the quinces, core and slice fairly finely, and immediately submerge in the water to stop them going brown.

Heat to boiling point and then simmer slowly, on a heat diffuser, for about 2½ hours. As the sugar slowly caramelises, the quinces will turn a wonderful dark red colour. Then liquidise in a food processor and strain through a fine nylon sieve to give a pink, quite thick quince purée. You can put it through finer and finer sieves if you want a clear liquid for jellies, but for blancmanges it is not necessary.

You need 250ml/1 cup/8fl oz for a 625ml/2½ cups/20fl oz blancmange. The rest you can freeze in containers to use later.

To make quince blancmange:

Metric	US	Imperial	
250 ml	1 cup	8 fl oz	*Quince juice*
250 ml	1 cup	8 fl oz	*Whole milk*
2½ tbsp	2½ tbsp	2½ tbsp	*Cornflour*
2 tbsp	2 tbsp	2 tbsp	*Sugar*

Mix the quince juice and the milk together first and then make exactly as the cornflour blancmange on p.66.

Trifle

It seems that the British can become fiercely provoked, even to the point of letter-writing, when the recipes of their favourite foods are defined. A specialist food magazine, *Petits Propos Culinaires*, innocently published a recipe for a celebratory trifle for its fiftieth edition. It contained jelly, cornflour and vanilla essence. The sky fell in and the magazine was flooded with mail for months, so we are cautious in committing ourselves to a recipe for a trifle (minus jelly, cornflour and vanilla essence, of course).

This recipe is adapted from a number of sources.

Trifle, ices and jellies

Metric	US	Imperial	
110g	4oz	4oz	*Naples biscuits or boudoir biscuits*
4 tbsp	4 tbsp	4 tbsp	*Strawberry jam*
125ml	½ cup	4fl oz	*Sherry or Madeira*
			EGG CUSTARD:
375ml	1½ cups	12fl oz	*Whole milk*
375ml	1½ cups	12fl oz	*Cream*
110g	½ cup	4oz	*Sugar*
6	6	6	*Egg yolks*
1	1	1	*Vanilla bean*
½ tsp	½ tsp	½ tsp	*or vanilla extract*
			SYLLABUB:
1	1	1	*Lemon*
110g	½ cup	4oz	*Sugar*
250ml	1 cup	8fl oz	*Wine or cider*
4 tbsp	4 tbsp	4 tbsp	*Brandy, Madeira or sherry*
625ml	2½ cups	20fl oz	*Whipping/heavy cream*

Spread the biscuits with the jam, break them up and put them into a large (1·8 litre/7 cup/3pt) glass serving bowl. Pour in the sherry or Madeira a little at a time until the biscuits are completely soaked.

Make the egg custard exactly as for the custard in Rich French vanilla ice-cream (p.108). Pour the custard, while still warm, over the soaked biscuits. Allow to cool.

Make the syllabub according to the recipe for Everlasting Syllabub (p.73). When completely cool, pour the syllabub over the custard and decorate with ratafia biscuits or tiny macaroons and nuts – but, please, not glacé cherries or glacé angelica or hundreds and thousands.

Syllabub

Apparently, syllabub was originally made by milking the cow directly into a bowl of cider, wine or verjuice. However, recent experiments by Ivan Day, with the help of an obliging cow, have confirmed that either tastes have changed considerably since the seventeenth and eighteenth centuries or many of the recipe writers had never tried the recipe. As recipe plagiarism was rife at that time, this may well have been the case. Helen McKearin writing in *The Glass Circle* (issue no.5) analysed 167 different recipes from 1655 to 1865 and found many were faithful repeats of the same one. Syllabub, however, divides into two basic types – simple, and everlasting or whipped.

The basis of syllabub is that an acid – cider, ale, wine, verjuice (or other acidic liquid) – is added to milk or cream. This causes it to curdle and separate. With simple syllabubs, the liquid would be drunk and the curdled cream (which was usually sweetened with sugar and sometimes flavoured) would float on the top to be eaten with a spoon. With everlasting syllabubs, they do not separate, and many more exotic colours, flavours and perfumes were used to flavour them, including fruit juices, flower waters, cloves, ambergris, musk and perfumed comfits.

There were many designs of syllabub glasses. Some had spouts and were similar to posset pots (p.89); they are now highly sought after by collectors. Syllabub was also frequently served in jelly glasses. There is still much discussion about the use of these various types of glass.

Simple syllabub

This recipe is from John Nott's *The Cook's and Confectioner's Dictionary*, published in London in 1733.

Metric	US	Imperial	
110g	½ cup	4oz	*Sugar*
250ml	1 cup	8fl oz	*Cider*
			Nutmeg, grated to taste
625ml	2½ cups	20fl oz	*Whipping/heavy cream*

Dissolve the sugar completely in a small amount of boiled water and allow to cool completely. Pour the cider into a bowl and add the sugar syrup and some grated nutmeg. Add the cream and stir, then leave to separate for about 2 hours in a cool place.

Lift off the curdled cream with a skimmer, pour the liquid into tall glasses, then carefully lay the curdled cream on top of the liquid.

The type of heavy-based Italian glasses used for bitters is ideal. Cut a straw in half and put that in the glass so you can drink the liquid. Sprinkle sugar on top of the curdled cream and serve with a spoon.

Everlasting, or whipped syllabub

Why syllabubs are almost never seen on menus today is a mystery. It is the ideal dessert as it is easy to make and keeps for 4–5 days in a refrigerator. Inexplicably, the only one we have found at a restaurant in the last five years was simply not worth eating.

It is one of the finest English desserts and a revival of syllabubs is long overdue. We have tried many recipes and think that this one is the best.

Metric	US	Imperial	
1	1	1	Lemon
110g	½ cup	4oz	Sugar
250ml	1 cup	8fl oz	Wine or cider
4 tbsp	4 tbsp	4 tbsp	Brandy, Madeira or sherry
625ml	2½ cups	20fl oz	Whipping/heavy cream

Peel the skin from the lemon, making sure that none of the white pith is attached. Put this with the sugar, wine or cider, plus brandy, Madeira or sherry, in a bowl, and allow to marinate overnight.

The following day remove the peel and add the cream slowly, while whisking continuously until the mixture will hold soft peaks. Take great care not to overbeat if using mechanical whisks; if in doubt use a balloon whisk and do it by hand. Transfer to tall glasses of about 70ml/¼ cup/2½ fl oz capacity and fill them to the brim.

Grate a little nutmeg on the top and keep at least 6 hours or overnight in the fridge before serving. Decorate with a sprig of rosemary or a twist of lemon peel.

Mrs Raffald suggests adding whipped syllabub on top of glasses that are half filled with wine, some white and some red. To serve you can also pour a little cream on the top of the syllabub.

Syllabub makes a wonderful topping to a trifle (p.70).

Fools

This is yet another English dessert that has almost disappeared. In his dictionary of 1598 the Italian, Florio describes the fool as 'a kinde of clouted creame called a foole or a trifle in English'.

The idea that the name is derived from the french 'fouler', to crush, is not only baseless, but inconsistent with the early use of the word. The Norfolk fool is probably the nearest to the original, and was not unlike a trifle. John Nott described it as a sort of pudding made with layers of manchet (bread) alternating with layers of egg custard flavoured with mace and cinnamon and covered with sliced dates and sugar.

In her *The Art of Cookery made Plain and Easy*, published in 1747, Hannah Glasse includes a Westminster fool that is also made with manchet, and quite similar to a trifle. We have adapted a recipe for gooseberry fool from Hannah Glasse's book.

Metric	US	Imperial	
550g	1¼lb	1¼lb	Gooseberries
110g	½ cup	4oz	Sugar
250ml	1 cup	8fl oz	Whipping/heavy cream

Half cover the gooseberries with water and gently simmer until soft, remove and drain in a colander, liquidise and then sieve to remove skins and seeds. You will be left with a fine pulp. Add the sugar a little at a time, as gooseberries vary enormously; you want to add just sufficient to make them edible, but not sweet. Chill thoroughly.

Beat the cream until soft peaks form and then fold into the gooseberry purée. You may fold in completely or leave streaks of cream and gooseberry to produce a more interesting effect.

You can replace the cream with an equal quantity of egg custard and add some nutmeg to the finished fool. Almost any other soft summer fruit can be substituted for the gooseberries in this recipe.

Serve in individual glasses, well chilled, with crisp shortbread biscuits.

Eton mess

The earliest record of this dish at Eton College seems to have been in the 1930s when it was sold at the Sock Shop – that is, the tuck shop. It was made of either strawberries or bananas, with ice-cream and cream according to Bernard Ferguson's 1938 book, *Eton Portrait*.

Sometime after this, meringue was added to the mixture, resulting in a combination of three of the most sublime textures and flavours known to man. Despite help from the archivist at Eton College, we have not been able to discover the origin of either the name or the recipe.

Metric	US	Imperial	
250 ml	1 cup	8 fl oz	*Whipping/heavy cream*
450 g	1 lb	1 lb	*Strawberries, washed and hulled*
4	4	4	*Meringues, individual*

You may substitute the strawberries with the same weight of peeled bananas.

Whip the cream until it will hold soft peaks, halve (or quarter if very large) the strawberries and break the meringues up into small pieces. Mix the whole lot together in a bowl and share it with as few people as possible!

White leach

The word 'leach' is a medieval culinary term meaning a slice. There were many kinds of leach including the Lombard, a spiced sausage of pork, diced fruits and almonds, and dry leach, a kind of gingerbread made with dates. By the Tudor period, white leaches were being made, using milk scented with rose water or almond milk jelly. These were cut into large cubes and coated with gold leaf to make one of the most luscious and glittering of all delicious sweetmeats served at the after dinner banquet in royal palaces and noble households.

They are surprisingly simple to make, with numerous variations. In the recipe below orange flower water can be substituted for the rose water. As for adding colouring, do so if you must, but the natural clear, white colour seems to have more elegance than even the most delicate tints.

Metric	US	Imperial	
625 ml	2½ cups	20 fl oz	*Whole milk*
5 leaves	5 leaves	5 leaves	*Leaf gelatine*
4 tsp	4 tsp	4 tsp	*or powdered gelatine*
110 g	½ cup	4 oz	*Sugar*
1½ tbsp	1½ tbsp	1½ tbsp	*Rose water*

Note: Be sure to buy a really good quality rose water or orange flower water (see useful addresses, p.140)

Lightly oil (use tasteless oil or, if you can get it, almond oil) a shallow rectangular tray (approx 20 × 10 cm/8 × 4 in). You can use any shape of dish or plastic box, as long as the depth of the leach is about 2·5 cm/1 in.

Warm the milk to around 60°C/140°F, dissolve the leaf gelatine or sprinkle in the powdered gelatine and stir until it is completely dissolved. Stir in the sugar and the rose water. Pour into the dish and leave to set.

Turn the leach out on to a damp cloth and cut into 2·5 cm/1 in squares and arrange these in a chequer-board pattern on a serving dish, so that it can be eaten with the fingers. Do not serve directly from the fridge, as the cold spoils the flavour; serve at room temperature.

Almond milk

There is considerable discussion about the use and origins of almond milk. Almonds have a high fat content and will, when pounded with water, make an excellent sweet, almond-tasting milk. Early recipe books always mention Jordan almonds, which in fact came from Spain. Almonds store well over winter, so the milk could be produced quickly at any time. For medieval Christians, forced by the Church to observe days of abstinence, almond milk really was a 'Godsend'. It enabled them to have luxurious food without using cow's milk, thereby getting around the ecclesiastical regulations.

Almonds were simply pounded in a mortar and mixed with water, heated and then wrung through a cloth.

Metric	US	Imperial	
450g	1 lb	1 lb	Almonds (skinned)
1 litre	4 cups	32 fl oz	Water
			Sugar, to taste

If you are in a hurry, put the almonds in a food-processor and process until they are a fine powder. Heat the water to boiling point, add half to the almonds and process until completely mixed.

Add the rest of the water and sugar to taste. Allow to cool. Work through a fine sieve and chill until needed.

Almond milk can be substituted for any milk in any of the cold dessert recipes.

One or two bitter almonds were often added to the Jordan almonds, but these are now difficult to find and are, in fact, illegal in the USA. You can add a couple of drops of bitter almond essence (available from Culpepper, see useful addresses p.140) as this really improves the almond flavour. However, if you are using actual bitter almonds, which are freely available in Italy and Spain, make sure that you boil the mixture briefly after adding the sugar.

If after you have sieved the milk, it is grainy, you can pass it through a coffee filter.

Chapter 5
SAVOURIES AND BUTTERS

Savouries

The savoury is a peculiarly English course, considered a stimulant to the digestion. Savouries reached the height of their popularity during Victorian and Edwardian times when they were frequently served in place of cheese at dinners; to serve both was unusual. They still enjoy a loyal following in gentlemen's clubs and at formal banquets. In the introduction to her *Book of Cookery* published in 1888, Agnes B. Marshall describes the savoury course:

> I have yet to speak of savoury entremets, which are now so generally served, both at large and small dinner parties, either in lieu of sweets or in addition thereto. Many persons eschew sweets either from questions of taste or health, or from the tendency which food of a saccharine nature has to produce obesity. A little cheese to assist the digestion, as the saying is, and still holds its own among the mass of the population. Such, indeed, is the simple germ from which the savoury course at a dinner has sprung, and still preparations, in which some cheese of distinctive character, such as Parmesan and Gruyere, &c., figures, are among the most popular dishes for terminating the repast.

She lists no fewer than 37 recipes in her original 1888 edition and 57 in her larger cookery book published in 1891.

Anchovy cream

Anchovy, mustard and cheese were the main ingredients of savouries, and this anchovy cream is used in many of the recipes. Make sure you mix the aspic according to instructions on the packet, and allow to cool.

Metric	US	Imperial	
6	6	6	*Anchovies*
1 tbsp	1 tbsp	1 tbsp	*Oil, olive or corn*
1	1	1	*Egg yolk, hard-boiled*
¼ tsp	¼ tsp	¼ tsp	*Pepper*
few drops	few drops	few drops	*Red colouring (optional)*
125 ml	½ cup	4 fl oz	*Aspic jelly, mixed and cooled*
125 ml	½ cup	4 fl oz	*Single/light cream*

Wash the oil from the anchovies and bone if necessary, add the oil, the hard-boiled egg yolk, the pepper and the colouring if used and pound in a mortar until smooth. Add the aspic jelly and sieve if necessary. Whip the cream until thick and then mix the purée into the cream. Chill in the fridge until cold. Serve on toast or small biscuits.

Welsh rarebit

Probably the best-known savoury but one where high quality ingredients really pay off. Use a rinded Cheddar cheese that is quite acidic; do not use processed cheese. With the right ingredients you are in for a real treat. The result will be nothing like you get in cafés and restaurants.

Metric	US	Imperial	
2	2	2	White bread, thin slices
			Butter, to spread
225g	8oz	8oz	Cheddar cheese
2 tbsp	2 tbsp	2 tbsp	Whipping/heavy cream
1 tsp	1 tsp	1 tsp	Mustard, English mixed
1/4 tsp	1/4 tsp	1/4 tsp	Pepper

Cut the bread into squares, removing the crust, and toast on both sides. Butter well and keep hot on a warmed plate.

Cut the cheese into very thin slices and put into a thick saucepan with the cream, mustard and pepper. Heat, stirring all the time, until the cheese has melted and the mixture is like cream.

Pour the cheese mixture over the bread and brown quickly under a hot grill. Traditionally, a salamander was used to brown the top, but a grill is much more convenient.

Buck rarebit

The origin of the name is unknown; perhaps it was considered that bucks (spirited, rather than elegant men) would prefer this version of a Welsh rarebit.

Make a Welsh rarebit exactly as above, but serve it with a poached egg on top.

Scotch woodcock

Metric	US	Imperial	
2	2	2	White bread, thin slices
			Butter, to spread
4 tbsp	4 tbsp	4 tbsp	Anchovy cream
			SAUCE:
2	2	2	Egg yolks
4 tbsp	4 tbsp	4 tbsp	Whipping/heavy cream
3 tbsp	3 tbsp	3 tbsp	Butter
¼ tsp	¼ tsp	¼ tsp	Pepper
4 tbsp	4 tbsp	4 tbsp	Parsley, chopped

Toast the two slices of bread (stale slices are best) and butter well on both sides. Spread one side with anchovy cream (p.78), place the other piece of toast on to make a sandwich and press well together. Cut into strips about 5cm/2in long and 2·5cm/1in wide. Arrange them in a circle on a heated dish and pour over the sauce.

To make the sauce, combine the egg yolks, cream, butter and pepper in a double saucepan or a bowl in a saucepan suspended over boiling water. Stir constantly until the mixture is thick and creamy but take care not to overcook to the scrambled egg stage. Add the chopped parsley, stir and pour over the miniature sandwiches.

Opposite: Ham, Green and Mustard butters (pp.85 and 87).

(*Robin Weir/Andreas von Einsiedel*)

Sardines with anchovy cream

The humble tinned sardine was once considered a great luxury. Fishermen in southern Brittany preserved the sardines by cooking the fish in butter and storing them in clay pots. This produced a much better and more delicate sardine than if they had been salted and dried.

In 1824 Joseph Colin established a sardine-canning plant at Nantes. He followed the same principle as the Breton fishermen, but substituted olive oil for the butter. Sardine-canning remained a French monopoly for about fifty years, despite the efforts by many nations to copy the process. French sardines were always, and still are, considered by connoisseurs to be the very finest. Although the French frowned on the English habit of serving tinned sardines hot, they make a wonderful savoury. Make sure you buy quality sardines in olive oil – anything else will be a disappointment.

Sardines were such a highly prized food that wonderful silver, ceramic and glass containers were developed to hold the tin from which the sardines were served on the table. The idea of sardines being served straight from the tin at table seems very odd today, but these containers – some quite beautifully decorated, and, regrettably, others crude and vulgar – now fetch surprisingly high prices at antique and collectors' fairs around the world.

Metric	US	Imperial	
1	1	1	Tin of French sardines in olive oil approx 175g/6oz
3	3	3	White bread slices
			Freshly ground black pepper, to taste
			1 recipe anchovy cream (pp.78–9)

Take the sardines out of the tin and carefully, using a pointed knife, remove the bone. Re-form by replacing the top fillets. Remove the crusts from the bread and cut into rectangles that are slightly larger than the sardines. Toast the bread lightly on both sides, then place a complete sardine on each piece of toast, grind a little pepper on the top and put them under the grill for about 2 minutes. Remove, and pipe the anchovy cream in a pattern on the sardine. Serve at once decorated with fresh parsley.

Opposite: My Lord of Carlisle's sack posset (p.90).
(*Robin Weir/Andreas von Einsiedel*)

Escalopes of eggs

A simple recipe from Mrs Marshall's *Book of Cookery* (1888), which makes a really delicious savoury.

Metric	US	Imperial	
3	3	3	*Eggs, hard-boiled*
			1 recipe anchovy cream (pp.78–9)
			Cucumber or 3 gherkins for garnish
			Chopped parsley for garnish

Hard-boil the eggs for no longer than 12 minutes, then plunge them into cold water. Prolonged boiling will make them discolour.

Remove a small slice from opposite sides and then slice through the middle lengthwise. This will ensure that each half will sit flat on the plate without rocking. Using a forcing bag, put a rosette of anchovy cream in the centre of each half egg, enough almost to cover the yolk.

Using either cucumber or gherkin, or both, cut small match-stick thickness shreds about 2·5cm/1in long and stick about four of these into each rosette.

Sprinkle with chopped parsley and serve.

Pastry ramekins for the cheese course

Another favourite at Georgian and Victorian dinner parties were the pastry ramekins – light, cheese-flavoured morsels which could be eaten with a fork, keeping the fingers dry and clean ready for the desserts to follow.

Metric	US	Imperial	
175g	6oz	6oz	*Puff pastry*
85g	3oz	3oz	*Cheese, (Cheshire, Cheddar, Stilton or Parmesan), grated*
1	1	1	*Egg yolk, beaten*

Preheat the oven to 220°C/425°F/gas mark 7/FO 200°C.

Roll out the pastry to form a 30cm/12in square and sprinkle this with half the cheese. Fold the pastry into three and roll out square again. Turn the pastry through 90 degrees, sprinkle it with the remaining cheese, fold it into three, and roll it out once more. Brush the pastry with beaten egg, cut into mouth-sized pieces. Arrange these on lightly greased baking sheets and bake for 15 minutes. Serve hot on a folded napkin.

Anchovies with Parmesan

After training in the kitchens of the Duke of Newcastle, under the renowned 'Monsieur de St Clouet', William Verral took over The White Hart at Lewes in Sussex in 1742. Here he provided both everyday meals and finer French cuisine for the gentry, especially during the races, assizes and county elections. They probably enjoyed the following dish, which was published in Verral's *A Complete System of Cookery* of 1759. 'This seems to be but a trifling thing', he wrote, 'but I never saw it come whole from the table.'

Metric	US	Imperial	
2	2	2	White bread slices
3 tbsp	3 tbsp	3 tbsp	Melted butter or olive oil
6	6	6	Anchovy fillets
4 tbsp	4 tbsp	4 tbsp	Parmesan cheese, grated
			Juice of an orange or lemon

Remove the crusts from the bread and cut into 6 fingers, 7·5 × 2·5 cm/3 × 1 in. Fry them in the butter or oil to a golden brown. Place them on some kitchen paper, put an anchovy fillet on each piece of bread, sprinkle with Parmesan cheese and place under a hot grill until the cheese has melted. Remove from the heat, sprinkle them with the orange or lemon juice, and serve immediately on a hot plate.

Savoury butters

Butters blended with a variety of ingredients to enhance their flavour and colour were a popular feature of the finest Victorian and Edwardian cookery. They were ideal for garnishing the most elaborate dishes, being arranged in pats, or piped on to a glazed boar's head, for example. They were also ideal for service at breakfast, luncheon or dinner, where they could either be spread on bread, toast or biscuits, or placed in small slices or pats on hot food, where they melted to form flavoursome accompaniments.

The following varieties are all suitable for modern use, but were taken from authentic Victorian recipes.

Anchovy butter

Metric	US	Imperial	
10	10	10	*Anchovy fillets*
85g	¾ stick	3oz	*Butter*
			Cayenne pepper, ground
			Nutmeg, ground

See method below.

Roller marker for butter

Epicurean butter

Metric	US	Imperial	
8	8	8	Anchovy fillets
85g	¾ stick	3oz	Butter
½ tsp	½ tsp	½ tsp	Chives, chopped
1 tsp	1 tsp	1 tsp	Tarragon leaves, chopped
4	4	4	Gherkins, chopped finely
2	2	2	Egg yolks, hard-boiled,and finely chopped

See method below.

Green butter

Metric	US	Imperial	
50g	2oz	2oz	Parsley leaves, scalded and drained
85g	¾ stick	3oz	Butter
50g	2oz	2oz	Anchovy fillets, washed

See method below.

Ham butter

Metric	US	Imperial	
50g	2oz	2oz	Cooked ham
85g	¾ stick	3oz	Butter
1	1	1	Egg yolk, hard-boiled
			Pepper, to taste
few drops	few drops	few drops	Red colouring

See method below.

Horseradish butter

Metric	US	Imperial	
3 tsp	3 tsp	3 tsp	*Horseradish, grated*
85g	¾ stick	3oz	*Butter*
¼ tsp	¼ tsp	¼ tsp	*Cayenne pepper*

See method below.

Lobster butter

Metric	US	Imperial	
110g	4oz	4oz	*Lobster meat, cooked*
4	4	4	*Anchovy fillets, washed*
85g	¾ stick	3oz	*Butter*
½	½	½	*Egg yolk, hard-boiled*
			Pepper, to taste
few drops	few drops	few drops	*Red colouring*

See method below.

Maitre d'hotel butter

Metric	US	Imperial	
2 tbsp	2 tbsp	2 tbsp	*Parsley leaves*
85g	¾ stick	3oz	*Butter*
2 tbsp	2 tbsp	2 tbsp	*Lemon juice, strained*

See method below.

Mustard butter

For steaks and hot fish.

Metric	US	Imperial	
85g	¾ stick	3oz	*Butter*
2 tsp	2 tsp	2 tsp	*English mustard, mixed*
2 tsp	2 tsp	2 tsp	*French mustard, mixed*
			Juice of 1 lemon, strained
1 tsp	1 tsp	1 tsp	*Tarragon vinegar*

See method below.

Method for all savoury butters

Finely chop the herbs, meat or fish and place them in a small bowl. Place the butter in a second small bowl, leave at room temperature for about half an hour to soften slightly, then beat with a wooden spatula or spoon until it becomes soft and pliable. At this stage add a little to the other ingredients, working them together against the side of the bowl until thoroughly mixed, then adding the remainder of the butter, incorporating it to form a smooth mixture.

Form the butter into a compact block, and place in its bowl in the refrigerator until it has become firm, and ready for moulding.

Wooden butter print

Chapter 6

NIGHTCAPS, WARMERS AND REFRESHERS

Hot milky drinks have always been considered to be both comforting and nourishing, and for this reason they have acquired a certain reputation as nursery and sick-room beverages, ideal for babies, children and invalids, but not very popular with healthy adults. This may well be the case today, when most homes, cars and trains have efficient heating, but previous generations, brought up in draughty houses with freezing bedrooms and accustomed to travelling hours on horseback or in unheated carriages through winter storms, fully appreciated hot drinks.

Ideally, they should be rich, smooth and alcoholic, producing a warm inner glow, thawing frozen limbs and relaxing both body and mind to induce a deep and dreamless sleep. The most important of these was the posset.

Simple possets, made by mixing boiling milk and ale together, and then stirring in white breadcrumbs, pepper and nutmeg, were made by seventeenth-century farmers for the men who stood half-submerged in streams when washing the sheep. Served in large wooden tubs at midday, this mixture revived their strength, and enabled them to continue their laborious work through the afternoon.

Indoor servants probably received posset made in the same way on winter nights: 'The surfeted Groomes doe mock their charge with Snores; I have drugg'd their Possets, that death and Nature do contend with them, Whether they live or die', cried Lady Macbeth, before sending her husband to murder Duncan. Similarly, Thomas Middleton's witch in his early seventeenth-century play of the same name: 'For the maide-servants, and girlies o'the house, I spiced them lately a drowsie posset'.

Posset made by working people for their own enjoyment was usually a mix of bread, milk and ale, especially in the northern counties of England. In the Peak District, rum, whisky, nutmeg, cloves, ginger, cream, lump sugar and toast were added for serving around Christmas. In the Lake District, posset included quartered figs, sugar, treacle and nutmeg, and was served on Good Friday. In Northumberland posset contained currant cakes, and was served to the bride and groom just before they went to bed, as described in Edward Chicken's *Colliers Wedding* in the early eighteenth century:

The posset made, the bride is led
In great procession to her bed ...
Thus spoke, she ran and catched the bowl,
Where currant cakes and ale did roll,
Then with a smile said 'Jenny lass,
Come, here's thy health without a glass',
Her arm supports it to her head,
She drinks and gobbles up the bread ...
And some prepare t'undress the bride,
While others tame the posset's pride.

It was customary for the wedding ring to be dropped into the posset. The bride and groom would taste it first, after which the lads and lasses tried to fish out the ring. The first one to succeed could hope to be the next to get married.

Treacle posset enjoyed a widespread reputation for easing the symptoms of the common cold. Hot milk curdled by the addition of black treacle or molasses was recommended for this purpose until the 1950s, if not later. Possets prepared for the gentry and the aristocracy were usually much richer affairs, made by pouring scalding cream into warm mixtures of eggs and wine or ale, flavoured with nutmeg, mace, cinnamon, rose water, etc. It was left by the fire, or in some warm place, to set as the smoothest, most delicate, flavoursome and alcoholic of all egg custards.

The vessels in which posset was made and served, known as posset pots or cups, were always of the highest quality; one writer in 1606 described 'Posset Cuppes carv'd with libberd's [leopard's] faces and Lyons heads with spouts in their mouths to let out the posset Ale.' Some were made of colourful slipware; others were in the glossy blue and white Delftware produced in London and Bristol, and other English factories (examples of these can be seen at Knole in Kent). Those of pewter could be 'furnished with two, three or four lateral pipes through which the liquid of the compound might be sucked by those who did not choose the bread'. The finest of all were made of silver, beautifully embossed and engraved, and supplied with matching covers and broad dishes to stand impressively on the dining-table. When using these pots, whatever the kind, it was customary for each person to take a spoon and scoop out the posset and eat it straight away, since the mixture would quickly separate into a smooth curd and a watery whey if any attempt was made to serve it out on to individual plates.

Scores of posset recipes survive in printed and manuscript recipe books of the last four centuries. The following were chosen to illustrate something of their range and quality. In addition, there is a selection of some of the other milk-based drinks, and some refreshers to wake you up again, before moving on to the ice-house.

My Lord of Carlisle's sack posset

James Howard, 1st Earl of Carlisle, was a favourite of James I of England, who travelled to Paris in 1624 to help negotiate the marriage between Charles, the Prince of Wales, and the French princess, Henrietta Maria. Five years later he retired from politics and devoted the rest of his life to lavish hospitality, which presumably included the following posset.

It is a typical recipe of the period, the ingredients and methods being very similar to those written down in numerous family recipe books of the seventeenth century. The original version included both ambergris and musk to give it a fine perfume, but these have been omitted here since they are not to be found in modern food shops.

Metric	US	Imperial	
9	9	9	Egg yolks
4	4	4	Egg whites
325 ml	1¼ cups	10 fl oz	Dry sherry
¼ tsp	¼ tsp	¼ tsp	Cinnamon, ground
¼ tsp	¼ tsp	¼ tsp	Mace, ground
¼ tsp	¼ tsp	¼ tsp	Nutmeg, grated
1 litre	4 cups	32 fl oz	Single/light cream
175 g	¾ cup	6 oz	Sugar, granulated

Beat together the egg yolks, egg whites, sherry and spices, and gently heat them in a large pan, stirring constantly until warm, but not thickened.

In another pan heat the cream and sugar together until it rises to a full boil, then pour from a good height into the warm egg and sherry mixture. Allow to stand in a warm place for a few minutes, sprinkle a little sugar over the surface and serve.

Snow posset

From the seventeenth century it has been the practice to make a separate froth, perhaps of egg white, sugar and cream, to lay on top of the semi-solid posset. Later versions incorporated beaten egg white into the posset, so that it would rise to the top and form a light, snow-like foamy curd. This version from *The Practical Housewife*, Anon, 1860, gives excellent results, but great care has to be taken during the final gentle heating, or the posset will separate and loose its smooth creamy consistency.

Metric	US	Imperial	
5 cm	2 in	2 in	Cinnamon stick
⅛	⅛	⅛	Nutmeg, ungrated
325 ml	1¼ cups	10 fl oz	Whole milk
2	2	2	Eggs, separated
3 tbsp	3 tbsp	3 tbsp	Sugar
150 ml	¾ cup	5 fl oz	Dry sherry

Simmer the cinnamon and nutmeg in the milk for 3–4 minutes. Beat the egg yolks in one bowl, and the egg whites, 1 tablespoon of the sugar and 1 tablespoon of the sherry in another.

Remove the cinnamon and nutmeg from the milk, slowly pour it on to the egg yolks while beating, and continue beating until it forms a smooth custard.

Pour the remaining sugar and sherry into a double saucepan or bain-marie and heat until warm, but not boiling. Whisk in the egg yolk mixture, then the egg whites, and continue to whisk over a gentle heat until the mixture below the froth is cooked to form a smooth custard. Remove the inner pan from the heat, dip the bottom of the pan briefly in cold water to stop it cooking, and wrap the pan in a towel for 5 minutes before serving.

King William's ale posset

The combination of ale and milk may not appear particularly appetising, but this recipe, presumably dating from the 1690s when William and Mary rebuilt their great suites of state and private apartments at Hampton Court Palace, gives very good results.

Metric	US	Imperial	
4	4	4	*Eggs*
625 ml	2½ cups	20 fl oz	*Single/light cream*
325 ml	1¼ cups	10 fl oz	*Strong brown ale*
110 g	½ cup	4 oz	*Sugar, granulated*
¼ tsp	¼ tsp	¼ tsp	*Nutmeg, grated*

Beat the eggs in a bowl and pour through a strainer into a double saucepan or a bain-marie. Beat in the remainder of the ingredients and heat gently, stirring continuously (the bottom may cook very quickly) until it has thickened slightly to form a smooth custard. This will occur just before it reaches simmering point.

Dip the bottom of the inner pan briefly in cold water to stop it cooking, then wrap it in a towel for 5 minutes before serving.

Treacle posset

This simple posset was traditionally believed to ease a bad cold.

Metric	US	Imperial	
325 ml	1¼ cups	10 fl oz	*Whole milk*
4 tbsp	4 tbsp	4 tbsp	*Sherry*
2 tbsp	2 tbsp	2 tbsp	*Treacle, black or molasses*

Pour the ingredients into a saucepan and heat gently, stirring continuously, until the mixture reaches boiling point and forms a soft curd. Pour into a mug and drink while the posset is still hot.

Apple posset

For centuries breadcrumbs or sponge-biscuit crumbs had been used to thicken possets, but this Victorian recipe shows how the old traditions continued.

Metric	US	Imperial	
450g	1lb	1lb	Cooking apples
2	2	2	White bread, 5mm/¼in slices
625ml	2½ cups	20fl oz	Whole milk
3 tbsp	3 tbsp	3 tbsp	Sugar, demerara
1 tsp	1 tsp	1 tsp	Ginger, ground
3 tbsp	3 tbsp	3 tbsp	Water

Place the apples in a baking tin with the water and bake at 180°C/350°F/gas mark 4/FO 170°C until soft, about 30–40 minutes.

Remove the crusts from the bread, place them in a saucepan with the milk, sugar and ginger, and cook, stirring continuously, until perfectly smooth.

When the apples are cooked, place them in a sieve over a bowl, and rub the pulp through to form a smooth purée.

Pour the bread and milk mixture into a warm bowl, stir in the apple purée, and serve at once.

Egg flip

Back in the eighteenth century, flips made by heating a mixture of beer, spirits and sugar with a hot iron were extremely popular, particularly with sailors. By the late Victorian and Edwardian period, it was virtually identical to egg-nog, in which eggs were beaten into hot beer, cider, wine or spirits, but made with hot milk. The following comes from Georgina, Countess of Dudley, a friend of Edward VII.

Metric	US	Imperial	
1	1	1	Eggs
1 tsp	1 tsp	1 tsp	Sugar
250 ml	1 cup	8 fl oz	Whole milk
1 tsp	1 tsp	1 tsp	Brandy

Lightly beat the egg, just to break it, and pour it through a sieve into a large mug, then beat it with the sugar to form a froth. Heat the milk until it is hot, but not boiling, and pour it, while beating, into the egg mixture. Finally stir in the brandy and serve.

Curried milk

In the late Victorian period, the teetotal movement began to make everyone aware of the 'demon drink'. Whole sections of society, such as the Methodists, gave up all beers, wines and spirits, which came to be seen as causes of great evil. For those who wanted a good warming drink, 'wholesome beverages' were devised, this particular example being recommended for those 'who may require to go abroad on very cold raw mornings, and will be much better, nay, entirely supersede, the use of ardent spirits'.

Metric	US	Imperial	
250 ml	1 cup	8 fl oz	Whole milk
1 tsp	1 tsp	1 tsp	Sugar
½–1 tsp	½–1 tsp	½–1 tsp	Curry paste

Pour the milk into a saucepan, heat until nearly boiling, then stir in the sugar and curry paste. Serve at once.

Milk punch

Punch, a mixture of wine or spirits, sugar, lemon juice, spices and water, first became popular in England in the 1630s. By around 1700 it had been discovered that the addition of boiling milk made a significant improvement, forming a fine curd which helped to filter the punch to perfect clarity, while the remaining whey made it very smooth and well flavoured. The following recipe from *The Practical Housewife*, Anon, 1860, entitled 'Milk Punch for Christmas Day', declares: 'This is the best recipe we have ever seen or used.' It really is good, producing an incredibly smooth and delicate lemon-flavoured liquor which is deceptively strong, and should be treated with respect.

Metric	US	Imperial	
3	3	3	*Lemons*
200 g	1 cup	7 oz	*Sugar, granulated*
500 ml	2 cups	16 fl oz	*Water*
375 ml	1½ cups	12 fl oz	*Rum*
125 ml	½ cup	4 fl oz	*Whole milk*

Using a potato peeler, peel the yellow zest from the lemons and place in a large bowl. Squeeze the lemons, sieve the juice and pour on to the zest. Stir in the sugar, water and rum. Heat the milk to boiling point, pour it over the ingredients, then cover the bowl and leave in a cool place for 24 hours.

Line a sieve with two or three layers of butter muslin, place over a jug, and filter the punch through the muslin, then pour it into a clean bottle. Cork and keep in a cool place until required. Serve it cold, either in glasses or by ladling it from a punch bowl.

Milk lemonade

Milk lemonade is restorative after exertion, as well as being refreshing on a hot summer's day.

Metric	US	Imperial	
3	3	3	*Lemons*
125 ml	½ cup	4 fl oz	*Water, boiling*
110 g	1¼ cups	4 oz	*Castor or ultra-fine sugar*
625 ml	2½ cups	20 fl oz	*Dry white wine*
1·75 litres	7½ cups	60 fl oz	*Whole milk*

Peel off the outside lemon skins, being careful that none of the pith is attached, and put it into a large bowl. Pour on the boiling water and leave overnight in the fridge. In the morning add the lemon juice from the three lemons, the sugar and the wine. Taste and add more sugar if it is too bitter. Boil the milk and add it to the lemon mixture, stirring all the time. Allow to cool, then strain through a strainer lined with muslin. It may take more than one straining to get the lemonade clear.

You may add 125 ml/½ cup/4 fl oz of sherry, or more, to liven up the proceedings if you wish.

Iced coffee

Coffee, which makes the politician wise
And see all things with his half shut eyes

Alexander Pope

Cooling Cups and Dainty Drinks by William Terrington, published in 1869, suggests that you make your coffee using the proportion 25 g/2 tbsp/1 oz of ground coffee to 250 ml/1 cup/8 fl oz of boiling water. This should be percolated and then refrigerated until completely cold.

Iced coffee should be served in a tall glass with ice-cubes added and milk or cream passed in a jug separately, so that each person can make it as white as they wish. It usually tastes better with sugar.

Iced tea

*The secret to making good iced tea is **never** to use hot water, as this dissolves the tannin and makes a bitter tea. Put 4 teaspoons of leaf tea (or 4 teabags) and 1 pint of cold water in a jug and leave to infuse for at least 24 hours.*

Serve in a tall glass with ice cubes and a slice of lemon.

Regent's punch

This punch was reputed to be the favourite of the Prince Regent.

Metric	US	Imperial	
1 bottle	1 bottle	1 bottle	*Champagne*
1 bottle	1 bottle	1 bottle	*Hock*
125 ml	½ cup	4 fl oz	*Dry sherry*
125 ml	½ cup	4 fl oz	*Pale brandy*
4 tbsp	4 tbsp	4 tbsp	*Rum*
125 ml	½ cup	4 fl oz	*Lemon juice, freshly squeezed*
4 tbsp	4 tbsp	4 tbsp	*Curacoa*
1 litre	4 cups	32 fl oz	*Green Tea*
1 bottle	1 bottle	1 bottle	*Seltzer water (soda water)*
			Sugar, to taste

Mix all ingredients together in a large bowl. The instructions say you should then 'ice to the utmost'.

Part Two
THE ICE-HOUSE

Today, we take the refrigerator for granted. Virtually every home has its own fridge and freezer, while refrigerated warehouses and shop cabinets ensure that perishable foods remain in good condition. As a result, ice-creams, sorbets, meats, fish, vegetables and some fruits are now readily and cheaply available throughout the entire year, instead of being seasonal delicacies, available only in bottles or cans, or as a result of the skilled expertise of head gardeners.

It was the introduction of efficient, virtually labour-free electric and gas-operated fridges into large households between the wars, and into smaller ones in the 1950s and 1960s, that made frozen food accessible to everyone. Before this, domestic ice-preservation was an extremely troublesome affair, while ice-making could be carried out only on an industrial scale.

The use of ice for cooling drinks probably originated in the Middle East, ice-houses being built in Mesopotamia some 4,000 years ago. The Bible (Proverbs 25: 13) records: 'As the cold of snow in the time of the harvest, so is a faithful messenger to them that send him; for he refresheth the soul of his masters.' The Greeks, Romans and Moors continued the tradition, and ice-houses were being built in France by the thirteenth century.

It was not until 1619, however, that James I had a 'snow-pit' dug at Greenwich Palace. This was England's first purpose-made structure in which the snow and ice of winter could be preserved for use during the hot summer months.

These early pits were sunk into the ground, lined with straw, then filled with foot-thick layers of snow separated by narrow layers of straw. A conical thatched roof over the top provided adequate insulation, while a drainage channel in the base carried off any melt-water, ensuring that the ice remained in good condition. Virtually identical examples were still being constructed in the nineteenth century, as at the 1834 ice-house at Scotney Castle in Kent, but by this time most ice-houses were large permanent structures, featuring numerous improvements.

From the late seventeenth century, the use of the ice-house spread from royal circles to the aristocracy and gentry. Frequently located on slightly rising ground, between parkland lake or pond and the house, they could be almost invisible, a covering mound of tree- and shrub-planted earth serving both as insulation and as an attractive landscape feature. A doorway facing away from the heat of the sun led into a passage fitted with two doors, the space between them providing additional insulation. Next came the chamber itself, its masonry walls tapering from a dome-vaulted roof down to the round, concave base, at the bottom of which was a wood or stone grating that covered the entrance to the drain.

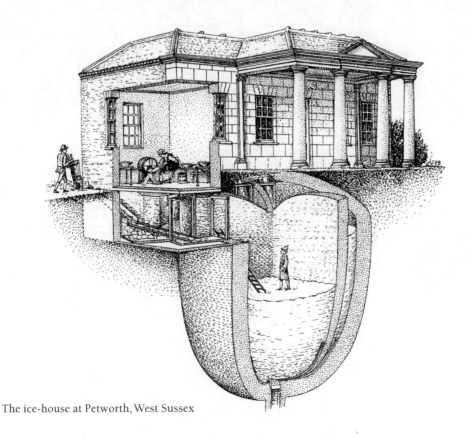

The ice-house at Petworth, West Sussex

Ice-houses of this type are to be seen at many houses, such as Powis Castle in North Wales, Hatchlands Park and Ham House in Surrey. Each example has its own particular characteristics: some have cavity walls, others feature loading holes in the roof, or vermin-proof traps in the drain. At Attingham Park in Shropshire, the ice-house has a rectangular barrel-vaulted chamber, surrounded by an insulated corridor, while the one at Petworth is completely buried below the dairy and is so large it had to be divided into three chambers, each with its own loading chute.

On some estates, the ice-house was incorporated into elaborate architectural schemes. At West Wycombe Park in Buckinghamshire the 1759 ice-house is entered through a broad three-arched flintwork façade and is topped by a tall, hexagonal Temple of the Winds. The ice-tower at Penrhyn Castle is even more

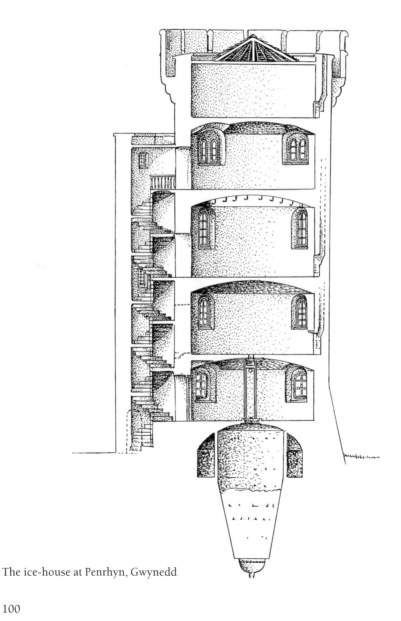

The ice-house at Penrhyn, Gwynedd

impressive, measuring over 70 feet high and topped with battlements designed as if to withstand a full-scale siege. Built around 1830, it has a 23-foot deep ice-house in its basement, an entrance at ground level for the gardeners to put in the ice, and a winch on the first floor to wind it up ready for use.

To fill the ice-house, most estates waited until a thick layer of ice had formed on a convenient stretch of water. Mallets were then used to break it up next to the bank, and, perhaps working from boats, into large mobile sheets. Iron-tipped poles could then pull the ice towards the bank, where it was broken into pieces, scooped out with sieves mounted on long handles, and barrowed or carted up to the ice-house. Before being packed inside, it was pounded into small pieces and then compacted into a solid mass within the chamber. Hot water and salt were sometimes poured on at this stage to help the ice form into a single solid block, which greatly extended its long-term preservation. Straw was still packed between the ice and the walls of the chamber, and sometimes between the pairs of doors in the corridor, to provide the maximum degree of insulation. Packed in this way, the ice could last throughout an entire season.

Ice breaking

Although meat and fruit could be preserved in the ice, this was not a common practice. Since the ice was essentially pond or river water, it was impure, unfit for human consumption. Its main purpose was for cooling a variety of foods and drinks.

Where ice was needed in the kitchen or confectionery, it was usually brought up by the gardeners and placed in an ice-box, a large wooden chest entirely lined with an insulated metal casing. From here, it would be taken out as required, and packed into a variety of utensils, along with quantities of salt, which formed a freezing mixture, and rapidly reduced its temperature. For making ice-cream, for example, it was packed into a wooden tub that surrounded the deep pewter freezing pots. The frozen ice-cream was then pressed into pewter moulds and placed within an ice-cave – a miniature freezer with hollow base, top, walls and door, all filled with the ice/salt freezing mixture. Jelly moulds were packed into bowls of ice to speed up the setting time, butter was placed on ice-cooled plates before being moulded, and desserts were placed in beautiful porcelain ice-tureens to keep them cool on the dining-table. Bottles of wine were cooled by being thrust into ice-filled pails and cellarettes, and some Georgian decanters had internal pockets which contained the ice while still keeping it separate from the liquor.

Ice was in particular demand in London, where no private or public entertainment would be considered complete without iced drinks and desserts. There was little opportunity in the city for gathering and storing fresh ice, so commercial suppliers, usually professional confectioners, were established in the late eighteenth century. As local supplies were outstripped by demand, ice began to be imported from overseas, where colder winters and clean unpolluted waters were supplied by nature.

Ice safe

From 1817 ice from Greenland and Norway was being shipped into the London docks, followed in 1842 by supplies from the United States. At first, the American ice attracted little attention, but then the Wenham Ice Company of Boston set up an ice-vault in the Strand and presented a large block of ice to Queen Victoria and Prince Albert at Windsor. They were so impressed with its clarity and purity that they arranged a regular supply, assuring an immediate boost in the company's sales.

The ice supplied by the ice-man came in large blocks, some measuring 53 × 53 × 38 cm/21 × 21 × 15 in, these being sawn into smaller blocks ready for use in refrigerators and ice-boxes. These devices, introduced during the 1840s, were timber-framed cupboards, lined with zinc or even glazed ceramic tiles, which incorporated recesses into which the ice blocks could be inserted, and wire shelves on which plates and dishes of perishable food could be kept delightfully cool and fresh during the summer months. The provision of ice still remained an expensive and troublesome business, however, especially in the countryside, distant from rail delivery services, etc., where ice-houses still had to be filled from local lakes.

On arrival at London's docks, Norwegian and American ice was transferred via the Regent's Canal to a series of enormous ice-houses around Paddington and King's Cross, some of them holding up to 1,500 tons in chambers cut 82-feet deep into the ground. From here, supplies were delivered by cart to all parts of the metropolis. By around 1900, after almost fifty years in the business, Carlo Gatti and his successors had established a clear monopoly of the ice trade, importing over 200,000 tons of Norwegian ice each year, with stores of 30,000 tons at the Norwegian lakes just to satisfy any unexpected demand. His yellow horse-drawn delivery carts, later replaced by lorries, were still delivering 15,000 tons of ice in the 1970s, but by this time it was produced using huge commercial ice-making machines.

Domestic refrigerators began to be introduced by the 1920s. Over the next forty years ice progressed from being a costly luxury, available only to the few, to being a cheap commodity available to all. The effect on diet has been considerable, enabling us to enjoy seasonal delicacies all the year round.

Ices

The history of ice-cream is fascinating, if only because the accepted facts melt away when examined. There are all sorts of popular myths quoted about the origins of ice-cream, most of which seem to have been introduced by the Victorians: how Marco Polo brought it from China; how Catherine de Medici introduced it to France; and how Charles I was supposed to have had his own personal ice-cream-maker – all wonderful stories, but sadly there is not a scrap of historic evidence to substantiate them. In fact, the latest research shows that Marco Polo didn't introduce ice-cream (or pasta) to Europe and, indeed, probably never even went to China!

The earliest evidence of anything approaching ice-cream being made was in China in the Tang period (AD 618–906). Buffalo, cow or goat milk was heated and allowed to ferment. This fermented milk was then mixed with flour for thickening and camphor (now used as an insect repellent) for flavour and 'refrigerated' before being served. King Tang of Shang had a staff of 2,271 people, including 94 ice-men.

The earliest methods of freezing foods needs some explanation. Freezing was achieved by mixing salt with ice, which reduces the freezing point and makes it quite easy to achieve temperatures lower than –14°C. Just who discovered the process is unknown, but it was probably the Chinese. It was written about in India in the fourth century and the first technical description of ice-making using various chemical salts was by an Arab medical historian, Ibn Abu Usaybi (AD 1230–70).

However, the process did not arrive in Europe until 1503, in Italy, where it was considered a chemist's party trick, using a mixture of various acids, water and chemical salts. Freezing was first used for food when water ices (sorbets) appeared in the 1660s in Naples, Florence, Paris and Spain. In 1694 ices made with sweetened milk first appeared in Naples. In England 'Iced Cream' was served at a banquet for the Feast of St George at Windsor Castle in 1671. It was such a rare and exotic dish that only the guests on Charles II's table had 'one plate of white strawberries and one plate of iced cream'. All the other guests could only watch and marvel at what the royal table was eating. It is not surprising that such a new and very different food should capture the attention of all who encountered it. In a short time, such was the interest and demand for ice-cream that wealthy people built ice-houses on their estates.

But what was ice without the cream? Such a rare and expensive food was only to be found on the tables of the high and mighty, so it is not surprising that ice-cream making was a closely guarded secret, for the knowledge of how to make it would have been a meal ticket for life. In such circumstances it was not until 1718 that the first recipe on how to 'ice cream' was published in English. This was a simple recipe using cream, either plain or sweetened, that was frozen and not agitated during the freezing. It would produce a very icy, rough textured type of ice-cream. The technique of making a custard-based ice-cream using egg yolks started in France around the middle of the eighteenth century.

The Americans took to ice-cream with avid enthusiasm and set about mechanising its manufacture. The original method involved a pewter pot kept in a bucket of ice and salt, which had to be regularly hand-stirred and scraped from the side of the pewter pots with a 'spaddle' – a sort of miniature spade on a long handle. The resulting ice-cream was rich and delicious, but of a dense consistency and it proved hard work to achieve an even texture.

The process was simplified with the introduction of the ice-cream machine in 1843 to both England and America. This consisted of a wooden bucket filled with ice and salt and had a handle that rotated a central metal container holding the ice-cream. This churning ensured an even, smoother texture to the ice.

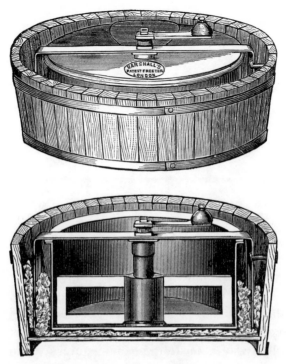

Marshall's patent freezer

At the end of the nineteenth century, the advent of mechanical refrigeration using electricity and gas made the ice-cream industry what it is today. No longer were huge quantities of ice necessary, and it became possible to transport and store ice-cream. Previously ice-cream had to be eaten within a few hours of being made because it required too much ice and salt to keep it frozen. Ice-cream quickly became a mass-market product and many of the old flavours became best-sellers. It is an interesting point that most of the flavours heralded as 'new inventions' by modern chefs can be found amongst the oldest recipes for ice-cream.

THE ICE-CREAM CONE
Most people think of the cone or cornet as the traditional way of eating ice-cream, and until recently it was claimed in the USA to be an American invention dating from the 1904 St Louis World Fair. As an American government official said in 1969, 'The ice-cream cone is the only ecologically sound package known. It is the perfect package.' Recent research, however, has shown that the edible ice-cream cone was an English invention. Although the edible cone itself can be traced back hundreds of years, the first recording of it being used for serving ice-cream was in 1888 in *Mrs Marshall's Book of Cookery*. Prior to that, ice-cream was either licked out of a small glass known as a penny lick or taken away wrapped in waxed paper referred to as 'hokey pokey' (words that are supposed to have come from the Italian '*ecco un poco*' – 'here is a little').

Chapter 7

ICE-CREAMS AND FROZEN PUDDINGS

Making ice-cream and ices

Making ice-creams and water ices is very simple as it requires so few ingredients – sugar, water, milk, cream and some flavouring. All you need is a freezer, a thermometer and a plastic freezer, sandwich or cake-box shape approximately $18 \times 15 \times 7$cm/$7 \times 6 \times 3$in to give a depth of mixture in use of 4 cm/$1\frac{1}{2}$in. An ice-cream machine is a luxury, and although you don't have to have one, it certainly makes it simpler and quicker.

All the equipment used must be scrupulously clean. Ideally, it should be put through a dishwashing machine or hand-washed in hot soapy water and rinsed in very hot water to remove every possible scrap of soap or detergent, and dried in the air, not with a cloth. Always refer to the manufacturer's instructions concerning cleaning machine parts. We always wipe the machine after washing with a cloth wrung out in a sterilising solution – the sort that is used for babies' bottles.

Ices, if badly handled, can provide an ideal breeding ground for all sorts of undesirable organisms, so cleanliness and speed of operation are important. Food-borne bacteria multiply most rapidly at temperatures around human blood heat. At temperatures below 10°C/50°F they are not killed, but the rate of multiplication slows considerably; at temperatures of 63°C/145°F they start to die. It is therefore important that as soon as a custard reaches 85°C/185°F it is cooled as fast as possible by plunging the bottom of the saucepan into a bowl of cold water and that the mixture is then transferred to the fridge as soon as possible.

First, check the temperature in your fridge and in your freezer. The fridge should be running at 4°C/39°F and the freezer at –18°C/0°F. Make sure that the fridge is not iced up; if it is, it will not work efficiently.

STILL-FREEZING
Still-freezing is the method of freezing without an ice-cream machine.

Having checked the temperature of your freezer, pour the chilled mixture into a strong polypropylene container (see dimensions above), cover with a lid and put in the coldest part of the freezer, preferably on the elements. Check after 1–1½ hours: the mixture should have frozen to a firm ring around the sides and base of the box, with a soft slush in the centre. Loosen the frozen ring from the sides of the box with a fork.

Either beat for a few seconds with a whisk or an electric hand-beater until the mixture forms a uniform slush, or quickly process in a food-processor to a uniform slush. Then replace the lid and immediately return the box to the freezer.

Repeat this process at least twice at intervals of 1–1½ hours. After the third beating, the ice will need freezing for a further 30–60 minutes to be firm enough to serve.

Alcohol-flavoured ices will take longer to freeze. It is better to make them the day before.

STIR-FREEZING
Stir-freezing is the method used when you have an ice-cream machine that has a moving paddle.

If you are using an electric machine, switch on and allow a pre-chilling time, if necessary. Pour in the mixture with the paddle revolving and churn for 10–15 minutes until frozen to a soft slush. If the ice is to be served immediately, continue churning for 5–10 minutes longer.

Do not go on churning an ice-cream in a machine longer than necessary as it will turn the cream to butter and ruin the ice-cream. Little flecks of butter will start to appear.

If you are using a hand-cranked machine using salt and ice, you are in for a lot of fun. Put the mixture in the machine and put in salt and ice in the ratio of 300g/1⅓ cups/11oz of rock salt or table salt to 3kg/10lb of crushed ice or ice cubes, while making the ice-cream. When it is made, use the same number of cups of salt to half the quantity of ice for hardening the ice. Hand-cranking ice-cream is hard work: the firmer the ice-cream, the harder it is to crank, so persuade someone energetic to do the work.

French *or* Rich French vanilla ice-cream

This is the basis of all custard-based ice-creams and can be varied between the two recipes.

FRENCH VANILLA ICE-CREAM

Metric	US	Imperial	
300 ml	1¼ cups	10 fl oz	*Whole milk*
1	1	1	*Vanilla bean*
100 g	½ cup	3½ oz	*Granulated sugar*
3	3	3	*Egg yolks*
250 ml	1 cup	8 fl oz	*Whipping/heavy cream (36% fat)*
Makes about			
800 ml	3¼ cups	26 fl oz	

RICH FRENCH VANILLA ICE-CREAM

Metric	US	Imperial	
375 ml	1½ cups	12 fl oz	*Whole milk*
1	1	1	*Vanilla bean*
90 g	⅓ cup	3¼ oz	*Granulated sugar*
5	5	5	*Egg yolks*
185 ml	¾ cup	6 fl oz	*Whipping/heavy cream (36% fat)*
Makes about			
800 ml	3¼ cups	26 fl oz	

Combine the milk, vanilla bean (split in half lengthways) and half the sugar in a medium-sized saucepan and bring to just below boiling point. Remove the pan from the heat, cover and leave aside for a minimum of 15 minutes to allow the vanilla flavour to develop.

Meanwhile, in a medium-sized heatproof bowl, combine the egg yolks with the remaining sugar and beat, preferably with an electric hand-mixer, until the mixture is pale and thick enough to hold the shape when a ribbon of mix is trailed across the surface. Bring the milk back to boiling point, then pour it in a thin stream on to the egg yolks and sugar, whisking steadily as the milk is added.

The bowl can now be placed over a pan of simmering water, or the custard can be returned to the saucepan, then placed on top of a heat diffuser so that it is not in direct contact with the heat. Only if you have an accurate thermometer and/or are confident that you will not overheat the sauce should you put the saucepan over a gentle direct heat. Use a small wooden spoon or spatula to stir the custard frequently. It will take anything from 5 to 30 minutes (depending on the thickness of the bowl or the pan) to thicken sufficiently, or to reach 85°C/185°F, and will need constant attention. If you do not have a thermometer, to judge if the custard is thickened sufficiently, remove the spoon and tilt the back of it towards you. If the custard forms only a thin film, try drawing a horizontal line across the back of the spoon. This should hold a clear shape. If not, continue cooking the custard until it coats the back of the spoon more thickly and holds a clear line.

As soon as the custard has reached the right temperature and thickened sufficiently, remove the pan from the heat and plunge the base a few inches into cold water. On no account should the custard be allowed to overheat or boil as the mixture will curdle. Leave to cool, stirring occasionally until the mixture feels as though it has never been heated.

Remove the pan from the cold water and transfer the custard to a bowl or jug, leaving the vanilla bean in the custard. Cover and chill in the fridge. The mixture can be left overnight at this stage. When ready, start the ice-cream machine. Use a teaspoon or the back of a knife to separate the tiny black vanilla seeds from the bean. Stir into the custard with the chilled cream. Either still-freeze (see p.106) or churn until the ice-cream is the consistency of softly whipped cream.

Cream ice-cream

Make as either of the above recipes, but omit the vanilla bean. Cream ice-cream is a wonderful flavour and can be put in croissants or used as you would use ice-cream or spread on sweet bread or rolls for a real treat.

Brown bread ice-cream

We were all surprised to find Brown bread ice-cream in Joseph Bell's 1817 *Treatise on Confectionary* (his spelling) when preparing for a dessert and ice-cream weekend at Syon House in 1997. Since then we have found it in Gilliers's *Le Cannaméliste français*, 1751, and Emy's *L'Art de Bien Faire*, 1768. Both these recipes use rye bread, which makes a wonderful nutty ice-cream. We had always assumed it was Victorian and did not realise that it was a popular Georgian recipe. It has a wonderful crunchiness that comes from the sugar and the breadcrumbs.

Metric	US	Imperial	
100 ml	1/3 cup	3 fl oz	*Wholemeal breadcrumbs*
500 ml	2 cups	16 fl oz	*Whipping/heavy cream (36% fat)*
185 g	1 cup	6½ oz	*Dark muscovado sugar*
Makes about			
700 ml	3 cups	24 fl oz	

We prefer to use unrefined dark muscovado sugar, as this gives a much more pronounced flavour. For a lighter ice-cream use unrefined demerara sugar. If you cannot get these sugars, use ordinary sugar and add up to 3 tablespoons of dark rum, one at a time, tasting to see what strength you prefer.

The recipe states 'add stale brown bread'. We suggest that you use wholemeal bread, grate it or put the crustless slices briefly in a food-processor and use the metal blade to make the crumbs. Toast the crumbs under a grill moving them around frequently until they are evenly browned. Don't use granary bread as the grains freeze hard and will break your teeth if you bite on them.

Add the toasted crumbs to the lightly beaten cream and sugar, then thoroughly chill, stirring occasionally. When ready, put into an ice-cream machine for about 20 minutes or still-freeze (p.106).

Clotted cream ice-cream

We always think of the wonderful dairy at Lanhydrock in Cornwall when making this ice-cream. Devonshire and Cornish clotted cream takes its flavour from the breed of cow and the time of the year that the cream is made.

Metric	US	Imperial	
375ml	1½ cups	12 fl oz	*Whole milk*
280g	1¼ cups	10oz	*Granulated sugar*
5	5	5	*Egg yolks*
125ml	½ cup	4 fl oz	*Clotted cream (55% fat)*
Makes about			
1 litre	4 cups	35 fl oz	

Combine the milk and half the sugar in a medium-sized saucepan and bring to just below boiling point. Now proceed according to the method for French vanilla ice-cream on p.108, to the point where the custard has reached the right temperature and/or has thickened sufficiently and the pan has been removed from the heat and the base plunged into a few inches of cold water.

At this stage immediately stir in the clotted cream and leave until cold before covering and transferring to the fridge to chill. When ready still-freeze (p.106) or start the ice-cream machine and pour in the custard. Because of the high fat content, churn this ice-cream only to the point where it is softly frozen and slightly thickened. If it is churned beyond this point, it is very likely to become buttery.

Quickly scrape into plastic freezer-boxes, level the surface and cover with grease-proof paper or freezer-film and a lid, label, then freeze. Serve in about an hour or, if frozen overnight, allow 15 minutes in the fridge before serving.

Double pan for Devonshire cream-raising

Clove ice-cream

Cloves were originally used by the Chinese to treat toothache and to sweeten the breath; you were expected to have a few cloves in your mouth when addressing the Emperor. Highly prized by the Romans, they became more popular and more widely used in Europe in the early sixteenth century when European sea voyages to the East Indies increased.

This is the perfect ice-cream to accompany rhubarb or, better still, apple pie, accompanied by a piece of Cheddar cheese.

Metric	US	Imperial	
250 ml	1 cup	8 fl oz	*Whole milk*
500 ml	2 cups	16 fl oz	*Whipping/heavy cream (36% fat)*
18	18	18	*Cloves*
6	6	6	*Egg yolks*
70 g	⅓ cup	2½ oz	*Granulated sugar*

Makes about			
850 ml	3½ cups	28 fl oz	

Combine the milk, cream and all eighteen cloves in the top half of a non-reactive double saucepan (i.e. not aluminium, unless coated). Sit this over a base pan of simmering water and allow it to reach just below boiling point. Turn off the heat, cover and leave to infuse for about 20 minutes.

Taste regularly to assess the strength of the clove flavour, bearing in mind that when frozen the taste will be milder. Also consider how you will serve it: apple pie or rhubarb crumble will take a stronger flavour of clove; a milder flavour is better if you are serving it with other ice-creams or sorbets.

Strain the cream to remove the cloves, and pour it back into the top half of a double saucepan. In a bowl whisk the egg yolks and sugar until foamy and stiff enough to support a trail of mix. Pour half the cream into the bowl in a steady stream, whisking constantly. Return the mixture to the rest of the cream and heat over a base pan of barely simmering water until the custard is thick enough to coat the back of a spoon. Strain the mixture into a bowl and cover with a sheet of buttered greaseproof paper to prevent a skin forming. Leave to cool, then chill in the fridge.

When ready, still-freeze (p.106) or churn in the ice-cream machine for 15–20 minutes. Serve within one hour. If frozen solid, allow 20–25 minutes in the fridge to soften.

Opposite: Parmesan cheese ice-cream (p.121).

(*Robin Weir/Andreas von Einsiedel*)

Cinnamon ice-cream

Make exactly as for clove ice-cream, but substitute about 30cm/12in of cinnamon sticks for the cloves. Break the sticks into smaller manageable pieces. If when you open the jar the aroma does not hit you, throw the cinnamon away as it is almost certainly stale. Do not use powdered cinnamon – it never really works. Cinnamon ice-cream is wonderful with apple or rhubarb, and equally good on its own.

Saffron ice-cream

Saffron (properly the dried stigmas of Crocus sativus) is a tricky ice-cream to get right. Very little saffron goes a very long way and an excess of the flavour can taste medicinal. However, correctly used, it has a wonderful flavour. It used to be most popular but has gone out of fashion. Fortunately, it is beginning to reappear in a few of the better restaurants.

Although once grown extensively in England, around Saffron Walden in Essex, saffron is now available only from importers. The quality can vary enormously so we always stick to strands of saffron (not the powder) from Valencia in Spain.

Strands are impossible to measure so we suggest a modest pinch. If the flavour is insufficient, allow the flavour to develop, preferably overnight, before adding more. Saffron is expensive, so if you overdo it, make a second batch of unflavoured ice-cream and mix the two together.

Make as for Rich French vanilla ice-cream (p.108), omitting the vanilla bean, up to the stage where the thickened custard is removed from the heat. At this point add the saffron strands, then leave aside to cool, before covering and chilling in the fridge overnight.

Still-freeze (p.106) or churn in an ice-cream machine. After churning, ensure that all the strands of saffron are scraped from the paddle and stirred into the ice-cream before freezing. Quickly put into a freezer-box, cover with greaseproof paper or freezer-film and a lid. Label, then freeze for a minimum of 2 hours until firm enough to serve. Once frozen solid, allow 20 minutes in the fridge to soften sufficiently before serving.

Opposite: Apple ice-cream and Ginger and lime sorbet (pp.118 and 133).

(*Robin Weir/Andreas von Einsiedel*)

Buttermilk ice-cream

This ice-cream probably came about as a result of a desire to use up buttermilk during butter-making. Fortunately, buttermilk is now available from good supermarkets, and the delicate distinctive flavour makes a wonderful ice-cream to eat on its own or with fresh fruit.

A delightful, clean-tasting, fresh-flavoured ice-cream with one disconcerting trait: it separates if the finished custard is left to stand before churning. However, this can be ignored, since it will not affect the ice-cream in any way.

Metric	US	Imperial	
3	3	3	Eggs
280g	1¼ cups	10oz	Granulated sugar
1	1	1	Vanilla bean
250ml	1 cup	8fl oz	Whipping/heavy cream (36% fat)
750ml	3 cups	24fl oz	Buttermilk
1 tbsp	1 tbsp	1 tbsp	Lemon juice

Makes about
1·25 litres	5 cups	40fl oz	

In a large heatproof bowl whisk together the eggs and sugar. Split the vanilla bean in half lengthways and put into a saucepan with the cream. Bring the cream to the boil then slowly pour into the bowl containing the beaten eggs and sugar in a thin stream, beating constantly.

Transfer to a double saucepan or position the bowl over a pan of barely simmering water and continue to heat, stirring frequently until the custard thickens or reaches 85°C/185°F. On no account should the custard be allowed to overheat or boil. Remove from the heat and lower the temperature of the custard quickly by setting the top of the double saucepan or the heatproof mixing bowl in cold water. Stir from time to time, testing the temperature. When it feels cold, remove the bowl, cover and chill in the fridge, preferably overnight.

When ready, remove the vanilla bean and, using a teaspoon, scrape the vanilla seeds from inside the pod; stir in the seeds and the buttermilk and the lemon juice. Still-freeze (p.106) or start the ice-cream machine and pour in the custard mix.

Leave to churn and freeze until the mixture is the consistency of thick cream; check after 10 minutes, as if it is left too long it will become buttery. Quickly scrape into plastic freezer-boxes, level and cover with greaseproof paper or freezer-film and a lid. Label and freeze overnight. Once frozen, allow about 30 minutes in the fridge to soften sufficiently to serve.

Goat's milk ice-cream

Goats were frequently kept so that the supply of milk continued both in the winter and when the cow or cows were 'dry'. Goats eat almost anything, and a lot less than a cow. Some people dislike the flavour of anything derived from goats. This ice-cream is for them; it retains just enough flavour to be recognised by those who enjoy it, but not enough to be noticed by those who do not. This is one of our top ten favourites and is wonderful on its own or served with red berry fruits.

Metric	US	Imperial	
375 ml	1½ cups	12 fl oz	Goat's milk
3	3	3	Egg yolks
100 g	½ cup	3½ oz	Granulated sugar
185 ml	¾ cup	6 fl oz	Whipping/heavy cream (36% fat)
Makes about			
750 ml	3 cups	24 fl oz	

Using the above quantities of goat's milk, egg yolks, sugar and cream, prepare, cook and freeze the ice-cream according to the method for making French vanilla ice-cream, p.108.

Brown sugar ice-cream

Now that unrefined sugar from Mauritius is available, it is possible to make ice-creams using unrefined sugars as the flavour. Although many of these sugars are too strong to use in sorbets, demerara, light muscovado and dark muscovado are all wonderful flavours for ice-creams.

Metric	US	Imperial	
325 ml	1¼ cup	10 fl oz	Whole milk
3	3	3	Egg yolks
100 g	½ cup,	3½ oz	Brown sugar
250 ml	1 cup	8 fl oz	Whipping/heavy cream (36% fat)
¼ tsp	¼ tsp	¼ tsp	Vanilla extract
Makes about			
750 ml	3 cups	24 fl oz	

Using the above quantities of milk, egg yolks, brown sugar and cream, prepare and cook a custard according to the method for making French vanilla ice-cream (p.108), adding the vanilla extract as the custard cools.

Rice ice-cream

Metric	US	Imperial	
110g	½ cup	4oz	*Pudding rice (short grain)*
500ml	2 cups	16fl oz	*Whole milk*
200g	1 cup	7oz	*Vanilla sugar*
500ml	2 cups	16fl oz	*Whipping/heavy cream (36% fat)*
Makes about			
1·25 litres	5 cups	40fl oz	

Rinse the rice, drain and put in the top half of a double saucepan with the milk and the vanilla sugar. Bring the rice to the boil, over direct heat, stirring constantly. Transfer to sit over the base pan of simmering water, cover and continue to cook for a further 40 minutes or until the rice is perfectly tender. Remove the top half of the pan from the heat and leave to cool, still covered, until the rice reaches room temperature, then transfer to the fridge to chill.

When ready, stir in the chilled cream and either still-freeze (p.106) or churn in the ice-cream machine for 15 minutes or until the mixture is the consistency of thick cream. Quickly scrape into a plastic freezer-box, cover with a piece of greaseproof paper or freezer-film and a lid, label and allow to freeze overnight.

Note: Because of the high starch content of this ice-cream, you must allow it up to one hour in the fridge to soften sufficiently to serve. Do not try to thaw at room temperature; the outside will melt while the centre remains rock solid.

Rice ice-cream with brandied fruit

This is a typical example of Victorian taste in ice-cream. They were very fond of piling in alcohol, spices and dried fruit. If you want to serve a plain rice ice-cream, for the best flavour we recommend cooking the rice as outlined in the recipe above. However, if you want to add crystallised fruits, nuts and brandy, the emphasis in flavour switches, so if you are in a hurry you can cheat and substitute a good quality canned, creamed rice-pudding. The flavour of the candied fruits will now come to the fore, so, if possible, try to buy whole cherries and the caps of orange, lemon and citron, rather than the brands of ready-chopped mixed peel which often seem strongly reminiscent of cleaning fluids, both in smell and taste.

Metric	US	Imperial	
90g	½ cup	3¼oz	Mixed crystallised fruits, finely diced
100ml	⅓ cup	3 fl oz	Brandy
250ml	1 cup	8 fl oz	Whipping/heavy cream (36% fat)
100g	½ cup	3½oz	Vanilla sugar
40g	¼ cup	1½oz	Almonds, toasted and chopped
425g can	15oz can	15oz can	Creamed rice-pudding
Makes about			
1 litre	4 cups	35 fl oz	

Put the finely diced crystallised fruits into a small saucepan with the brandy and bring to simmering point. Cover and continue to simmer very gently for 3–4 minutes, or until the peel is perfectly tender and about one tablespoon of liquid remains. Leave to cool, covered. Combine with remaining ingredients, stir well, cover and chill in the fridge.

When ready, freeze exactly as Rice ice-cream (p.116), scraping any pieces of fruit off the paddle and mixing them in when you put it in the plastic freezer-boxes.

Strawberry and sour cream ice-cream

Sour cream and strawberries are a pleasant surprise because they are not as sweet as an ordinary strawberry ice-cream.

Metric	US	Imperial	
100g	2 cups	3½oz	Strawberries
250ml	1 cup	8 fl oz	Whole milk
4	4	4	Egg yolks
200g	1 cup	7oz	Granulated sugar
250g	1 cup	9oz	Sour cream
Makes about			
1 litre	4 cups	35 fl oz	

Hull and wash the strawberries in cold water and dry them on a towel or kitchen paper. When dry, purée the strawberries and half the sugar, then chill in the fridge. Prepare a custard according to the method for making French vanilla ice-cream (p.108) and chill in the fridge.

When ready, add the sour cream and strawberry purée and churn the mixture in an ice-cream machine, or still-freeze (p.106).

Apple ice-cream

This recipe is adapted from Mrs Marshall's 1885 recipe for marmalade ice-cream. In the days before deep-freezes, supermarkets and the availability of fresh fruit all year round, fruit ice-creams made out of season used jam or marmalade.

This is a very quickly made ice-cream and uses ready-made, smooth, Bramley apple purée to obtain an amazingly good flavour with the minimum of fuss.

Metric	US	Imperial	
280g	1 cup	10oz	*Smooth Bramley apple purée*
500ml	2 cups	16fl oz	*Whipping/heavy cream (36% fat)*
30g	2 tbsp	1oz	*Castor or ultra-fine sugar*
1–2 tsp	1–2 tsp	1–2 tsp	*Lemon juice*
Makes about			
850 ml	3½ cups	30 fl oz	

Chill the apple sauce and cream in the fridge. When ready, combine the apple sauce, whipping cream and sugar and mix thoroughly, taste and add lemon juice if you think it is too sweet. Cool in the fridge again.

Churn the cooled mixture in an ice-cream machine for about 20 minutes or still-freeze (p.106). Then quickly scrape into plastic freezer-boxes, level the surface and cover with greaseproof paper or freezer-film and a lid, label, then freeze. Serve in about an hour, or, if frozen overnight, allow 20 minutes in the fridge before serving.

Note: This recipe can be adapted to make other flavours. Substitute the same quantity of good quality jam or marmalade for the apple purée. For example, to make apricot ice-cream, substitute the same quantity of good apricot conserve or jam for the apple purée. If the jam or marmalade has large pieces of fruit in it, liquidise quickly, as large pieces of frozen fruit are not always pleasant in an ice-cream.

Seville orange ice-cream from marmalade

Before the advent of freezers, jam, marmalades and preserves were frequently used for making ice-creams and sorbets because the only way fruits could be preserved was with sugar. Fruits were available only in their correct seasons, and transportation from warmer countries was impossible unless the fruits were preserved in sugar.

This recipe calls for 'smooth' marmalade and we suggest using Coopers Fine-cut Oxford Seville Orange Marmalade. Although Joseph Bell in his 1817 *Treatise on Confectionary* suggests straining it to remove the peel, we like the slight texture in the ice. Purists will probable wish to strain the marmalade mixture before freezing, or it can be liquidised with the orange juice at the start. Tiny specks of peel make the ice look more attractive.

Metric	US	Imperial	
310g	1 cup	11oz	*Marmalade*
1–2 tsp	1–2 tsp	1–2 tsp	*Orange juice*
500ml	2 cups	16fl oz	*Whipping/heavy cream (36% fat)*
2 tbsp	2 tbsp	2 tbsp	*Sugar, golden granulated*
Makes about			
1 litre	4 cups	35fl oz	

Combine the marmalade and orange juice and process in a food processor until the peel is only tiny specks. Then add the cream and sugar and process very briefly to mix well. Chill thoroughly. When ready, put the cooled mixture in an ice-cream machine for about 20 minutes or still-freeze (p.106).

If you want a really gutsy, full-flavour, marmalade ice-cream, use the same amount of Coopers Vintage Marmalade, but substitute 2 tablespoons of lemon juice for the orange juice and unrefined dark muscovado sugar for the unrefined golden granulated sugar. Make in exactly the same way, making sure that the marmalade and lemon juice are well processed to reduce the peel to tiny specks.

Savoury ice-creams

Savoury ice-creams, although popular in Georgian and Victorian times, have been almost forgotten. However, these are well worth trying.

Stilton cheese ice-cream

This ice-cream would have been served at the end of the meal in place of a hot savoury but nowadays can be used as a starter.

Metric	US	Imperial	
625 ml	2½ cups	20 fl oz	*Whole milk*
1	1	1	*Clove*
250 g	9 oz	9 oz	*Stilton cheese*
4 tbsp	4 tbsp	4 tbsp	*White port*
			Salt and freshly ground pepper
550 g	2 cups	1 lb 2 oz	*Fromage frais/fromage blanc*
Makes about			
1·3 litres	5½ cups	45 fl oz	

Bring the milk, with the clove in it, almost to boiling point in a double saucepan or, carefully, on the stove. Chop the cheese, having discarded the rind, into approximately 1cm/½in cubes. Add to the milk and stir over the heat until completely melted. Remove the pan from the heat and beat vigorously for about 30 seconds before adding the port. Taste and add salt or freshly ground black pepper if needed. Cool and then chill in the fridge.

When ready, remove the clove, and gently beat the fromage frais into the chilled mixture. Still-freeze (p.106), or churn in the ice-cream machine for about 8–10 minutes.

When frozen, allow about 20–25 minutes in the fridge before serving.

Cut into slices and serve with melba toast and a glass of port.

Parmesan cheese ice-cream

This is an adaptation from a recipe in Joseph Bell's 1817 *Treatise on Confectionary*.

Metric	US	Imperial	
500 ml	2 cups	16 fl oz	Whipping/heavy cream (36% fat)
110 g	½ cup	4 oz	Sugar, golden, granulated
110 g	1 cup	4 oz	Parmesan cheese (grated)
Makes about			
750 ml	3 cups	24 fl oz	

Carefully bring the cream to the boil with the sugar, stirring gently and constantly, remove from the heat and then add the grated Parmesan cheese, still stirring constantly, until it melts. Allow to cool.

Leave overnight in the fridge. The mixture will be firm enough to freeze in the morning. Scrape into a freezer-box, give it a good stir, level the ice and cover with greaseproof paper or freezer-film and freeze for at least 6 hours.

Serve this with fresh pears.

Note: Use only Parmigiano-Reggiano. Cheaper Parmesan cheeses are too greasy and rubbery and the ice cream will be grainy. Use golden granulated sugar that is unrefined and comes from Mauritius, as the ice-cream needs the flavour.

Crushing ice

Caviar/lumpfish roe ice-cream

This ice should be still frozen to keep the roe intact. Use of a machine breaks up the roe; this does not matter if red roe is used, but black roe looks singularly unappetising.

Metric	US	Imperial	
2	2	2	*Shallots or spring onions*
250 ml	1 cup	8 fl oz	*Sour cream*
50 g	2 oz	2 oz	*Caviar or lumpfish roe*
1 tbsp	1 tbsp	1 tbsp	*Lemon juice*
2 tbsp	2 tbsp	2 tbsp	*Vodka*

Makes about
| 350 ml | 1½ cups | 12 fl oz | |

Chop the shallots or onions very finely indeed, and mix them with the sour cream in a glass bowl. Add the caviar or lumpfish roe, keeping back one teaspoonful for garnish, then the lemon juice and the vodka and mix very carefully in order to preserve the caviar/lumpfish roe.

Still-freeze (p.106), stirring after the first hour of freezing. It can then be served an hour after stirring.

However, if fully frozen, allow about 20–30 minutes in the fridge before serving.

Serve with a very small ice-cream scoop with slices of lemon and toast. It used to be served in fish-shaped savoury bombe moulds.

Parfaits

A parfait is the ultimate ice-cream, light, delicate and creamy. The classic flavour is coffee, although parfaits made with sweet fortified wines or liqueurs are also wonderful. It is very rare to get a true parfait today, which is surprising as it is easy to make and does not require an ice-cream machine. However, you must follow the instructions exactly to make a perfect parfait. The maximum you should make each time, to ensure success, is twice the recipe below. If you want more than this, keep repeating this quantity. Parfaits are ideal as the centre for a bombe.

Coffee parfait

Metric	US	Imperial	
4	4	4	*Egg yolks*
1 tbsp	1 tbsp	1 tbsp	*Instant coffee*
185 ml + 2 tbsp	¾ cup + 2 tbsp	6 fl oz + 2 tbsp	*Sugar syrup (p.137)*
250 ml	1 cup	8 fl oz	*Whipping/heavy cream (36% fat)*

Makes about			
500 ml	2 cups	16 fl oz	

Ideally you need a thermometer, an electric hand-mixer and a double saucepan, but a large heatproof bowl which will sit snugly into a saucepan over water will serve nearly as well.

Put the egg yolks into the bowl and use the electric mixer to whisk them until light and pale. Dissolve the instant coffee in 30ml/2 tablespoons of sugar syrup by warming it slightly. Add the rest of the syrup and warm the coffee syrup to 30-40°C/86-104°F (around blood heat), then whisk this, a few tablespoons at a time, into the egg yolks. Now either position the bowl over, but not in, a saucepan of barely simmering water, or pour the mixture into the top of a double saucepan positioned over, but not in, scarcely simmering water. Cook, stirring regularly to make sure that the mixture is not overcooking at the base or in the angles of the pan. Heat either until the temperature reaches 85°C/185°F or until the mixture has thickened sufficiently to coat the back of a spoon. It will take 10-25 minutes.

Remove the mixture from over the water and pour into a large deep mixing bowl. Using an electric hand-beater, beat on high speed for about 1 minute. Then adjust the beater to medium speed and beat for a further 3-4 minutes. Finally, turn the speed to slow and beat for a further 5 minutes.

By this stage the volume will have increased by about 50 per cent and the mixture will be almost cold and thick enough to hold a ribbon trailed over the surface. Put the bowl holding the mixture and a second empty bowl, plus the whipping cream, in the fridge and leave to chill for at least 1 hour.

When ready, remove the empty bowl, pour in the chilled cream and beat until it forms soft peaks. Now remove the yolk/syrup mixture from the fridge and gently fold in the whipped cream in about four stages. When complete, pour into a plastic freezer-box, cover with greaseproof paper or freezer-film and a lid. Finally label and freeze for at least 2 hours. A parfait frozen solid will need about 15-20 minutes in the fridge to soften before serving.

Liqueur *or* fortified wine parfait

Any sweet fortified wine, dessert wine or liqueur makes a wonderful parfait. Our favourite is Cointreau, but port, sherry or Madeira are delicious, and some of the drier fortified wines are interesting.

Metric	US	Imperial	
4	4	4	Egg yolks
185 ml	¾ cup	6 fl oz	Sugar syrup (p.137)
250 ml	1 cup	8 fl oz	Whipping/heavy cream (36% fat)
1–4 tbsp	1–4 tbsp	1–4 tbsp	Liqueur or fortified wine
Makes about			
1·25 litres	5 cups	40 fl oz	

Make exactly as the previous recipe, sprinkling in the liqueur or fortified wine after folding in the second lot of cream.

Mrs Marshall's almond cornets

Unfortunately most people today have never ever tasted a real ice-cream cone. Glass cones were used in Naples from 1820, but Mrs Agnes Marshall was the first person in the world to suggest putting ice-cream in an edible cone or cornet, in 1888. This recipe for almond cornets is an adaptation of her recipe from *Fancy Ices*, 1894, and is not difficult to make. It is a world away from the modern cones, all air and powder with almost no flavour.

Metric	US	Imperial	
225 g	1½ cups	8 oz	Ground almonds
110 g	½ cup	4 oz	Castor or ultra-fine sugar
110 g	¾ cup	4 oz	Flour, plain
4	4	4	Eggs, medium
½ tsp	½ tsp	½ tsp	Vanilla extract
2 tbsp	2 tbsp	2 tbsp	Rose water

You will need to use non-stick baking trays. Wipe these with a pad of kitchen paper moistened with vegetable oil. You will also need 6 cream horn (conical) tins oiled inside and out.

Preheat the oven to 180°C/350°F/gas mark 4/FO 160°C.

In a bowl, beat together the eggs, vanilla extract and rose water. In a large separate bowl combine the almonds, flour and sugar, and stir until evenly mixed. Pour the egg mixture onto the dry ingredients and stir to form a stiff paste.

Measure three level tablespoons of mixture onto the greased baking tray and, using a small metal spatula, spread the mixture thinly and evenly in circles about 14-15cm/5¾-6in diameter. You can do this by eye as the circles will be trimmed later. There should be room for three circles on each baking tray, as they do not spread during the baking process.

Bake in the oven for 7-8 minutes or until small blisters form on the surface as the wafers lift themselves from the baking tray.

Now you will need to work quickly. Remove the tray from the oven and using a 14cm/5½in-diameter saucepan-lid or a plate as a guide, quickly cut out a neat circle from each wafer. Roll each one firmly around a cream horn tin to form a cornet shape then slip each one inside another tin to hold the cone shape while it finishes baking. Put them on a baking tray and return the cornets to the oven. Reduce the oven temperature to 160°C/325°F/gas mark 3/FO 140°C and bake for a further 10-11 minutes or until the cornets are tinged golden brown and crisp. They must dry out before they become too brown so watch them carefully until you get the measure of your oven. Remove from the oven and leave to cool with the tins in place. If the tins are removed when the cornets are hot they are likely to lose their round shape at the wide end of the cone.

Repeat with remaining mix; this mixture will make about 15 cornets in all. Fill with the ice-cream of your choice. Mrs Marshall used apple ice-cream and ginger sorbet to fill them and stacked them in a pyramid interleaved with fern, setting them on a white doily.

Chapter 8

SORBETS, SHERBETS AND GRANITAS

Although the sorbets and granitas in this chapter contain no dairy produce as such, their production was originally the responsibility of the dairymaid who made them in the cool conditions of her dairy. Only later was their production taken over by the confectioner if the household was sufficiently wealthy to support an extensive staff. The confectioner was always considered to be in a class well above the other kitchen staff, usually on a par with the chef or head cook. He (for it was usually a man) would have his own team of assistants and usually a location that had really good light needed for the intricate sugar work. For example, in Syon House in Middlesex, the home of the Dukes of Northumberland, the kitchens are in a separate building in case of fire, to the north of the house, whereas the confectionery is in the main house on the south-west side.

Water ices or sorbets first appeared in the 1660s in Naples, Florence, Paris and Spain. Known as *eaux glacées* or *acque gelate* or *eaux d'Italie*, they consisted of a simple mixture of water, sugar and flavouring, frozen hard. However the ratio of sugar to liquid was important: too much stopped it freezing, too little and it became a block of ice.

Rose water sorbet

Rose water is a clear distillation of red rose petals and has the intense perfume of its source. At its best, it tastes of an old-fashioned rose garden in full bloom, but at the same time it has a surprising spicy, smoky quality, which is why rose petals often marry well with some blends of China tea. You may need to search for the very best triple distilled rose water, and it will be expensive. Your nose will detect the cheaper versions, which are often reminiscent of some cosmetics well past their sell-by date. Our favourite is the rose water from the Santa Maria Novella pharmacy in Florence, now available in London and New York (see useful addresses p.140).

Metric	US	Imperial	
375 ml	1½ cups	12 fl oz	Sugar syrup (p.137)
375 ml	1½ cups	12 fl oz	Water
2 tbsp	2 tbsp	2 tbsp	Rose water
			Juice of 1 lemon, strained
Makes about			
875 ml	3½ cups	28 fl oz	

In a large measuring jug combine the sugar syrup, water, rose water and lemon juice, to taste. Chill thoroughly in the fridge.

When ready, still-freeze, (p.106) or churn in an ice-cream machine for about 5 minutes or until it becomes opaque and is firm enough to serve. To store, quickly scrape the ice into a plastic freezer-box and cover with a piece of greaseproof paper or freezer-film, label, then freeze. Once frozen solid, allow about 30 minutes in the fridge until it is soft enough to serve.

Orange-blossom sorbet

This is made with orange-blossom (or flower) water which is a distillation of orange flowers. Although the smell is somewhat reminiscent of cheap boiled sweets, it does wonders for both sweet and savoury foods. Avoid citrus flower waters and look for the mellow orange flower waters from Italy, France and North Africa. We use Acqua Di Fior D'Arancio from the Santa Maria Novella pharmacy in Florence, now available in London and New York (see useful addresses p.140), which we find wonderfully flavoured and reliable.

Metric	US	Imperial	
375 ml	1½ cups	12 fl oz	Sugar syrup (p.137)
375 ml	1½ cups	12 fl oz	Water
1 tbsp	1 tbsp	1 tbsp	Orange flower water
			Juice of 1 lemon, strained
Makes about			
875 ml	3½ cups	28 fl oz	

Follow the method for making rose water sorbet, substituting orange flower water for the rose water.

Herb sorbets

Unless you have fresh herbs available, don't try these sorbets. Dried herbs simply do not work.

You can use almost any herbs but choose one from the list below to get the most effective results.

These sorbets are delicious served as an alfresco starter on a hot summer's day.

Metric	US	Imperial	
			Herb (see below)
500 ml	2 cups	16 fl oz	*Sugar syrup (p.137)*
250 ml	1 cup	8 fl oz	*Water*
250 ml	1 cup	8 fl oz	*Dry white wine*
			Lemon juice (see below)

Makes about			
1 Litre	4 cups	35 fl oz	

HERBS AND LEMON JUICE:

	Herb	Lemon juice
15 g or 10 large leaves	*Basil*	3 tbsp
6 × 10 cm/4 in sprigs	*Mint*	2 tbsp
4 × 15 cm/6 in sprigs	*Rosemary*	3–4 tbsp
15 g or 25 leaves	*Pineapple sage*	2 tbsp
10 g or 4 × 5 cm/2 in sprigs	*Thyme*	2 tbsp

Rinse and dry the herbs, put into a non reactive saucepan (i.e. not aluminium, unless coated) with the sugar syrup and the water. Bring slowly to the boil. Remove the pan from the heat and add the wine. Cover and leave to cool. Chill overnight in the fridge. Strain, then add the lemon juice to taste.

When ready, still-freeze, (p.106) or churn in the ice-cream machine. It will take about 20 minutes to freeze to a soft slush. Quickly scrape into a plastic freezer-box and cover with a piece of greaseproof paper or freezer-film, label, then freeze for at least 1–2 hours before serving.

Note: It takes longer to freeze because of the alcohol in the wine. Once frozen solid it will need only about 10–15 minutes in the fridge to soften.

Opposite: Mrs Marshall's almond cornets (p.124).

(*Robin Weir/Andreas von Einsiedel*)

Lavender sorbet

Make sure that you have either grown the lavender yourself or you have bought culinary quality lavender. Do not use ordinary dried lavender or lavender sold for flower-arranging as it may have been sprayed with insecticides. If you cannot get good lavender, you can use a teaspoon of lavender tea.

The amount of lavender sounds very small, but four heads are all that is needed to make a most wonderful aromatic, delicate pink sorbet.

Metric	US	Imperial	
250 ml	1 cup	8 fl oz	*Sugar syrup (p.137)*
4	4	4	*Lavender heads*
			Juice of 1 lemon, strained
375 ml	1½ cups	12 fl oz	*Water*
Makes about			
750 ml	3 cups	24 fl oz	

Pour the measured syrup into a pan, add the lavender heads and slowly bring to the boil, then remove from the heat and add half the strained lemon juice. (Don't be surprised, it will turn pink.) Cover and leave to cool. Strain the syrup to remove the lavender, and add the cold water. Taste, and, if it seems too sweet, add the remaining lemon juice.

When ready, still-freeze, (p.106) or churn in the ice-cream machine for about 8–10 minutes until it is firm enough to serve. To store, quickly scrape into a plastic freezer-box and cover with a piece of greaseproof paper or freezer-film, label, then freeze. Once frozen solid, it will need only about 10–15 minutes in the fridge to soften sufficiently to serve.

Opposite: Ice-cream making equipment in the dairy at Ham House.
(*NTPL/Andreas von Einsiedel*)

Somerset cider sorbet

The perfect store-cupboard sorbet. It can be produced at little notice and always impresses. It requires no cooking and if you have the sugar syrup and cider ready in the fridge, you can have it made in minutes.

There is now a wide range of ciders available with which to experiment. We prefer a really dry cider as it seems to give a much better flavour to the sorbet. However, it is also good with a sweet cider. Serve this with apple ice-cream for a real treat (p.118), or, for a really hot day, make a cider float by putting scoops of cider sorbet in a large glass of cider. Serve with a long spoon and a straw.

Metric	US	Imperial	
625 ml	2½ cups	20 fl oz	*Dry cider*
375 ml	1½ cups	12 fl oz	*Sugar syrup (p.137)*
1 tbsp	1 tbsp	1 tbsp	*Lemon juice*
Makes about			
1 litre	4 cups	35 fl oz	

Chill the cider, add the syrup and the lemon juice to taste.

When ready, still-freeze, (p.106) or churn in the ice-cream machine for about 10–15 minutes until it is firm enough to serve. To store, quickly scrape into a plastic freezer-box and cover with a piece of greaseproof paper or freezer-film, label, then freeze. Once frozen solid, it will need only about 20 minutes in the fridge to soften sufficiently to be served.

Earl Grey (and other) tea sorbet

The secret to making any tea sorbets lies in the infusion. Recipes always tell you to add boiling water. **Don't!** Simply soak the tea in cold water overnight. This gives a good round flavour and none of the bitter tannin that is immediately released when tea-leaves are steeped in boiling water.

If you really must, use teabags, substituting 4 teabags for the tea-leaves.

Russian Caravan tea gives a good positive flavour. Japanese green tea has a wonderful delicate flavour, as do jasmine tea or Gunpowder Green. Lapsang Souchong and Darjeeling give a bold flavour suitable to serve with strong flavoured fruit, such as plums or damsons. Experiment with teas and various fruits; the taste combinations are a revelation.

Metric	US	Imperial	
3 tbsp	3 tbsp	3 tbsp	*Earl Grey tea-leaves*
625 ml	2½ cups	20 fl oz	*Water*
300 ml	1¼ cups	10 fl oz	*Sugar syrup (p.137)*
			Juice of 1 lemon, strained
Makes about			
1 litre	4 cups	35 fl oz	

Add the tea to the cold water, stir well and leave to steep in the fridge for 24 hours, stirring occasionally. Pour through a tea-strainer, discarding the tea-leaves or teabags. Then add the sugar syrup and the lemon juice to taste. Chill in the fridge.

When ready, still-freeze (p.106) or churn in the ice-cream machine for about 5–10 minutes until it is firm enough to serve. To store, quickly scrape into a plastic freezer-box and cover with a piece of greaseproof paper or freezer-film, label, then freeze. Once frozen solid, it will need only about 15–20 minutes in the fridge to soften sufficiently to serve.

Muscat *or* dessert wine sorbet

The success of this sorbet depends on the quality of the dessert wine that you use. This recipe is good using homemade wines, elderflower being particularly successful.

Metric	US	Imperial	
350 ml	1½ cups	12 fl oz	*Dessert wine*
250 ml	1 cup	8 fl oz	*Sugar syrup (p.137)*
250 ml	1 cup	8 fl oz	*Water*
			Juice of 1 lemon, strained
Makes about			
1 litre	4 cups	35 fl oz	

To the wine add the sugar syrup, water and strained lemon juice, to taste. Cover and chill in the fridge.

When ready, still-freeze (p.106) or churn in the ice-cream machine for about 8–10 minutes until it is just firm. Because the alcohol will impede the freezing, now put the sorbet into the freezer for about 1 hour so it becomes frozen hard enough to serve. To store, quickly scrape into a plastic freezer-box and cover with a piece of greaseproof paper or freezer-film, label, then freeze. Once frozen solid, it will need only about 15–20 minutes in the fridge to soften enough to serve.

Pomegranate sorbet

Try to pick pomegranates that have pink or crimson flesh, rather than those that are almost white. This will give the sorbet a wonderful fuchsia red colour. The flavour is delicious and works well served with fresh figs.

Metric	US	Imperial	
3 large or 4 small	3 large or 4 small	3 large or 4 small	*Pomegranates*
150g	¾ cup	5¼oz	*Castor or ultra-fine sugar*
3 tbsp	3 tbsp	3 tbsp	*Lemon juice, strained*
Makes about 625 ml	2½ cups	20 fl oz	

Halve and squeeze the juice from the pomegranates as you would any citrus fruit, using a lemon or grapefruit squeezer. Any debris retained should be transferred into a plastic sieve positioned over a bowl; then either manually squeeze the pulp or press it hard to extract the last of the juice. There should be about 500ml/2 cups/16 fl oz of juice. Stir the sugar and the lemon juice into the pomegranate juice until dissolved. Cover and chill in the fridge.

When ready, still-freeze (p.106) or churn in the ice-cream machine for about 10-15 minutes until it is firm enough to serve. To store, quickly scrape into a plastic freezer-box and cover with a piece of greaseproof paper or freezer-film, label, then freeze. Once frozen solid, it will need only about 10 minutes in the fridge to soften sufficiently to be served.

Sorbetières

Ginger and lime sorbet

There is nothing quite like the fresh taste of ginger and lime together. This sorbet is wonderful served with Apple ice-cream (p.118)

Metric	US	Imperial	
50g	2oz	2oz	Fresh ginger peeled
250 ml	1 cup	8 fl oz	Sugar syrup (p.137)
250 ml	1 cup	8 fl oz	Water
			Juice of 2 limes
			Zest of 1 lime

Makes about		
750 ml	3 cups	24 fl oz

Chop the peeled ginger into chunks, put into a food-processor and chop as finely as possible. Add the syrup and water and process again, briefly.

Bring to the boil in a non-reactive saucepan (i.e. not aluminium, unless coated), remove from the heat, add the lime juice, cover and allow to cool.

When ready, strain, if you do not want tiny pieces of ginger in your sorbet. We, however, prefer them left in as this gives the sorbet a delicious texture and a better look. Carefully scrub the skin of one of the limes and dry. Remove the zest with a zester and cut into pieces no longer than 5mm/¼in. If you do not have a zester, use a potato peeler to peel the lime and then cut in very fine strips with a sharp knife. Add the zest of the lime to the ginger mixture, taste and add more juice of lime if liked.

When ready, still-freeze (p.106) or churn in the ice-cream machine for about 8–10 minutes until it is firm enough to serve. To store, quickly scrape into a plastic freezer-box and cover with a piece of greaseproof paper or freezer-film, label, then freeze. Once frozen solid, it will need only about 10–15 minutes in the fridge to soften sufficiently to serve.

Sherbets

The word 'Sherbet' almost defies description, so mangled has it become by the influences of nations, legislation and ignorant usage. The word probably comes from the Arabic 'sharab' meaning a cold sweetened drink. Nowadays, a sherbet is usually a water ice containing a small amount of milk or cream, whereas a sorbet contains no dairy products. This is the definition accepted in most of the world. The US Food and Drugs Administration (FDA), however, has no classification for a sorbet. What everyone else calls a sorbet, the FDA call a water ice and they have an additional classification for sherbet (where the milk-derived solids must not be less than 2 per cent and not more than 5 per cent) and ice-milk (where the milk-derived solids must not be less than 11 per cent).

Earl Grey tea sherbet

Metric	US	Imperial	
3 tbsp	3 tbsp	3 tbsp	*Earl Grey tea**
375 ml	1½ cups	12 fl oz	*Water*
325 ml	1¼ cups	10 fl oz	*Sugar syrup (p.137)*
			Juice of 1 lemon, strained
250 ml	1 cup	8 fl oz	*Whole milk*
Makes about			
1 litre	4 cups	35 fl oz	

Make exactly as you would the sorbet (p.130), but add the chilled milk before freezing.

*If you must use teabags, use four, but don't tell anyone and choose a good quality brand.

Rose-petal sherbet

Rose-petal sherbet is a wonderful ice to serve on a hot summer's day, either on its own or for tea in the garden with shortbread.

If you cannot get roses, substitute 4 tablespoons of good quality rose water.

Note: You must use highly scented roses for this recipe which have not been treated – i.e. sprayed with insecticides.

Metric	US	Imperial	
150 g	¾ cup	5 oz	*Sugar*
150 ml	¾ cup	5 fl oz	*Water*
3	3	3	*Rose heads*
2 tbsp	2 tbsp	2 tbsp	*Lemon juice*
250 ml	1 cup	8 fl oz	*Whole milk*
Makes about			
500 ml	2 cups	16 fl oz	

Add the boiling water to the sugar, stir briefly to ensure the sugar has melted completely, then put in the rose petals, submerge them and allow to cool.

When cold, strain to remove the petals, add the lemon juice, stir well and then add the milk. Still-freeze (p.106) or churn in an ice-cream machine for about 10 minutes.

Orange-blossom sherbet

Make exactly as for the previous recipe, but substitute orange flower water for the roses or the rose water.

Noyau sherbet

Crème de Noyau, or Noyaux, is a peach-flavoured liqueur made from a selection of nuts and fruit kernels. Be careful not to get Crème de Noyeau, which is a pink or white almond-flavoured liqueur.

This sherbet is ideal with other ice-creams and sorbets, particularly plum and soft fruit flavours.

Metric	US	Imperial	
250 ml	1 cup	8 fl oz	*Sugar syrup (p.137)*
3 tbsp	3 tbsp	3 tbsp	*Crème de Noyau or Noyaux*
2 tbsp	2 tbsp	2 tbsp	*Lemon juice*
250 ml	1 cup	8 fl oz	*Whole milk*
1 drop	1 drop	1 drop	*Bitter almond extract*

Makes about
625 ml	2½ cups	20 fl oz

Mix the sugar syrup, Noyau and lemon juice together and chill.

When cold, add the milk, stirring the mixture briskly. Finally add the bitter almond extract, using a fine metal skewer. Taste, and, if liked, add another drop of extract. Either still-freeze (see p.106) or churn in the ice-cream machine for 15–20 minutes. When becoming firm, quickly scrape into a plastic freezer-box, cover with greaseproof paper or freezer-film and a lid. Label and put in the freezer for at least an hour. If frozen solid, it will need about 20 minutes in the fridge before it is soft enough to scoop.

Note: Bitter almond extract is available from Culpepper (see useful addresses p.140).

Sugar syrup

The sugar syrup used in all sorbets, granitas, parfaits and sherbets in this book is a simple combination of sugar and water.

We like to make a standard syrup which is then kept in the refrigerator to use when needed. This is easier than making small quantities of syrup for each recipe.

Metric	US	Imperial	
1 kg	5 cups	2lb 3oz	*Sugar*
1 litre	4 cups	35 fl oz	*Water*
Makes about			
1·6 litres	6²/₃ cups	55 fl oz	

Simply put the water, boiling straight from the kettle, into a large plastic jug, add the sugar and stir. It will dissolve immediately. Allow to cool and then refrigerate.

There is no need to boil the syrup, it simply evaporates the water and increases the concentration of sugar.

This syrup will keep for at least 2 weeks in the refrigerator.

We always use unrefined sugar from Mauritius for sugar syrups.

Making sugar cones

Granitas

The granita is one of the many wonderful dishes the Italians have given us. It is a coarse-textured, still-frozen, flavoured ice. A granita is basically a sorbet mixture with added water. Its origin is unclear but it is amazingly simple to make and the most refreshing of all the ices. All you need is a polypropylene sandwich or cake box, $25 \times 25 \times 8\,cm/10 \times 10 \times 3\,in$, and a strong fork. It must be no deeper, as this will take too long to freeze because of the amount of trapped air insulating the mixture.

The made mixture is put in the box, covered with the lid and frozen, preferably in the quick freeze part of the freezer. Freeze for an hour or until the liquid has formed an ice-ring around the edge of the box. Remove the box from the freezer and with the fork break up the ice, scraping it away from the edge and mixing together to make a uniform slush. Repeat this process every half hour for about $2\frac{1}{2}$ hours until the mixture forms a smooth consistency of identifiable ice crystals. A proper granita should have separate, almost 'dry' ice crystals. It is impossible to achieve this texture any other way, so do not resort to a food-processor.

When made, the granita will keep for 3 or 4 hours. If you have kept it in the freezer overnight, let it partially defrost and repeat the freezing sequence.

If you become a granita enthusiast, it is well worth getting a simple sacchrometer. This will enable you to make any flavour of granita you wish, provided the sugar density registers between 9°-10° Baumé (density 1·066-1·075) on the sacchrometer scale.

Almond granita

It isn't easy to get the almond flavour in a water ice, but if you use Orgeat, the French almond syrup used in cocktail-making, the flavour is fantastic. Nothing else seems to make such a respectable tasting granita, so it is worth the search for a French Orgeat. Using real almonds just produces a gritty ice with a nasty aftertaste.

Metric	US	Imperial	
250 ml	1 cup	8 fl oz	Sugar syrup (p.137)
125 ml	½ cup	4 fl oz	Orgeat
700 ml	2¾ cups	22 fl oz	Water, chilled
3 tbsp	3 tbsp	3 tbsp	Lemon juice
			Slivered almonds for decoration
Makes about			
1 litre	4 cups	32 fl oz	

Combine the chilled syrup, orgeat and water in a jug. Add 2 tablespoons of the lemon juice, taste and add the third if necessary. (Do not worry if it tastes a bit flat; the freezing and the texture will improve the granita out of all recognition.) Make according to the instructions for granitas.

Coffee granita

Wonderfully refreshing on a hot summer's day. Serve in the kind of glass used for Italian bitters drinks.

Metric	US	Imperial	
875 ml	3½ cups	28 fl oz	*Water*
200 g	1 cup	7 oz	*Granulated sugar*
3 strips, 2·5 × 1·25 cm	3 strips, 1 × ½ in	3 strips, 1 × ½ in	*Lemon peel*
5 tbsp	5 tbsp	5 tbsp	*Instant coffee*
2 tbsp	2 tbsp	2 tbsp	*Kahlua® (Mexican coffee liqueur)*
Makes about 500 ml	2 cups	16 fl oz	

Measure 250ml/1 cup/8fl oz of water into a small pan add the sugar and the strips of lemon peel. Bring to the boil and after 30 seconds, remove the pan from the heat and stir in the instant coffee, the rest of the water and the Kahlua® and allow to cool in the fridge. Remove and discard the lemon peel. When ready, make according to the instructions for granitas.

Serve in a glass with a spoon topped with softly whipped cream.

Irish coffee granita

Simply substitute Irish whiskey for the Kahlua®.

Herb granitas

You can make herb sorbets into herb granitas simply by adding 560ml/2¼ cups/18fl oz of chilled water, at the same time as the wine, to any of the recipes on page 128, and following the instructions for a granita.

Sources of drawings

Useful addresses

INGREDIENTS

Santa Maria Novella Pharmacy, UK
117 Walton Street
London SW3 2HP
Tel: 0171 460 6600
Fax: 0171 460 6601

Santa Maria Novella Pharmacy, USA
Takashimaya
693 Fifth Avenue
New York
NY 10022
Tel: 212 350 0591
Fax: 212 350 0192

Culpepper
21 Bruton Street
London W1X 7DA
Tel/Fax: 0171 629 4559

Culpepper Mail Order
Hadstock Road
Linton
Cambridge CB1 6NJ
Tel: 01223 894054
Fax: 01223 893104

Dean and Deluca
560 Broadway
New York
NY 10012
Tel: 212 226 6800
Fax: 212 226 2003

MAIL ORDER EQUIPMENT

Lakeland Plastics
Alexandra Buildings
Windermere
Cumbria LA23 1BQ
Tel: 015394 88100
Fax: 015394 88300

BOOKSHOPS

Books for Cooks
4 Blenheim Crescent
London W11 1NN
Tel: 0171 221 1992
Fax: 0171 221 1517

Selected bibliography

Acton, Eliza, *Modern Cookery,* 1845

Anon., *The Practical Housewife,* 1860

Bell, Joseph, *A Treatise on Confectionary,* 1817

Clark, Lady, of Tillypronie, *Cook Book of,* 1909

Emy, M., *L'Art de Bien Faire les Glaces d'Office,* 1768

Fairclough, Margaret, *The Ideal Cookery Book,* 1911

Garrett, Theodore, *The Encyclopaedia of Practical Cookery,* 1909

Glasse, Hannah, *The Art of Cookery made Plain and Easy,* 1747

Grigson, Jane, *English Food,* 1974

Kitchiner, William, *The Cook's Oracle,* 1817

Marshall, Agnes, *The Book of Ices,* 1885

Marshall, Agnes, *Cookery Book,* 1888

Marshall, Agnes, *Larger Cookery Book of Extra Recipes,* 1890

Marshall, Agnes, *Fancy Ices,* 1894

Massey, John and William, *Comprehensive Pudding Book,* 1875

Norwak, Mary, *English Puddings,* 1981

Nott, John, *The Cook's and Confectioner's Dictionary,* 1733

Raffald, Elizabeth, *The Experienced English Housekeeper,* 1769

Terrington, William, *Cooling Cups and Dainty Drinks,* 1869

Verral, William, *A Complete System of Cookery,* 1759

Index

Note: Page numbers in italics refer to the captions for photographs.